What Others Say about *No Time* ~~*es*~~

*As a mother whose daughter was .
member of the board of Parents of   'ou
from the bottom of my heart. I will   k to
others.*

Wai.   ....cer, M.D., Madison, Wisconsin

Thank you so much for your sensitive writing of No Time for Goodbyes. *I
wish you the best of luck in future endeavors.*

Joseph Biden, United States Senator. Delaware

*What a book! What a comfort! What insight!   This book must be made
available in all countries.*

Joan Isherwood, children killed, Cheshire, England

*For 15 months, your book stayed in my purse. Now I keep it by my bed.
Thanks so very much, Janice. Although I've never met you, you are the one
who gave me the strength to go on.*

Cindi Winkle, fiance killed, Aumsville, Oregon

*I lost all my family within three years and grief overwhelmed me. Thank you
so much for your book, which was sent by a friend. I wish you all the best for
your important work.*

Dr. Ruthmarijke Smeding, The Netherlands

*You have managed to put together a knowledgeable, compassionate and
factual book to help those of us who have been suddenly thrust into the
unwilling role of victims. God bless you for your insight and wisdom. I thank
you from the bottom of my heart for your lifeline.*

Patricia O'Connor, child killed, Jackson, New Jersey

*This book is invaluable for hospice counselors and for families grieving a
violent death. It adds priceless emotional and practical information about
grief.* No Time for Goodbyes *is rich with personal testament to the love and
courage of survivors.*

Joyce Dace-Lombard, grief counselor, Camarillo, California

No Time for Goodbyes *will become one of the books I most highly
recommend to any surviving family member. I never thought I would curl up
with a good book and spend most of the time crying.*

Donna Lamonaco, law enforcement husband killed, Brandywine, New Jersey

There is sound advice here, not only for those grieving a violent death but for those who want to comfort them.
Review in *Sydney Morning Herald,* Sydney, Australia

I want to thank you for putting into words the heartbreak and utter devastation one feels when a loved one has been suddenly taken from you.
Gloria Cook, child killed, Gibsonia, Pennsylvania

Ms. Lord provides excellent practical suggestions for coming to grips with grief and coping with the specific problems encountered.
Review, American Trauma Society

As part of our counseling program, we have discovered that No Time for Goodbyes *is very helpful in giving families tools to reach some resolution of their loss.*
Judy Batchelor, grief counselor, Detroit, Michigan

Why didn't I find your book two years ago? It seems like an eternity since I journeyed to that black pit of emotions within. Your words helped me realize how far I've come. At times when I feel the shadow of that time, I pick up your book and realize I am not alone.
Sue Look, friend killed, South Perth, Australia

This book should be in the hands of every victim of homicide. To my knowledge, there is no other resource that so touches this unique group of people.
Rhonda Anthony, MADD, Fresno, California

I couldn't make sense of this world any longer after my sister and her daughter were murdered. Your book helped me a great deal. Thank you for writing such a helpful book.
Sandra Mulcah, St. Paul, Minnesota

This is one of the best grief books I've read – and I've read them all!
Laurette Hupman, publishing consultant, Wilmette, Illinois

Your book is terrific! You're right on target about tragic death.
Lauri Ware, funeral director, Fort Worth, Texas

As a bereavement facilitator I've read a lot about grief and related topics.

When I read the dedication page in your book, I thought it might be different, and I wasn't disappointed. A spiritual warmth emits from its pages that is healing. I highly recommend it!

Mary Hammericksen, Seattle, Washington

NO TIME FOR GOODBYES

Coping with Sorrow, Anger, and Injustice
After A Tragic Death

NO TIME FOR GOODBYES

Coping with Sorrow, Anger, and Injustice
After A Tragic Death

By

Janice Harris Lord

Pathfinder Publishing of California
Oxnard, CA

NO TIME FOR GOODBYES

Published By:
Pathfinder Publishing
of California
3600 Harbor Boulevard, #82
Channel Islands, CA 93035, U.S.A.

Copyright 1987, 1988, 1991, and 2000 by Janice Harris Lord
First Printing 1987
Second Edition January 1988 Revised
Third Printing 1989
Third Edition 1990 Revised
Fifth Printing 1990
Fourth Edition 1991 Revised
Seventh Printing 1992
Eighth Printing 1993
Ninth Printing 1994
Tenth Printing 1995
Eleventh Printing 1996
Twelfth Printing 1997
Thirteenth Printing 1997
Fourteenth Printing 1999
Fifth Edition Printing 2000
Sixteenth Printing 2001
Seventeenth Printing 2001
Eighteenth Printing 2002

Library of Congress Cataloging-in-Publication Data
Lord, Janice Harris
        No Time for Goodbyes: coping with sorrow, anger, and injustice after a tragic death / by Janice Harris Lord – 5th ed.
        p. cm
        Includes bibliographical references and index
ISBN 0-934793-68-9 $12.95
1.   Bereavement – psychological aspects. 2. Violent deaths – Psychological aspects. 3. Grief. I Title
BFG575.G7L66 1991
155.9'37-dc20
        91-31702
        CIP
ISBN 0-934793-68-9

DEDICATION

To the countless victims of violence who dared to open their hearts to me and thereby carved into my heart a deepened capacity to care. I can never fully understand your pain, but I treasure your willingness to allow me to stand with you in your suffering.

ACKNOWLEDGEMENTS

Many people planted seeds throughout the years that blossomed into the fifth edition of this book. So many colleagues contributed to its evolution that it would be difficult to mention each by name. The victims who shared their stories with me breathed life into these pages. While I can never name them all, I will remember every one.

A major note of gratitude goes to Dr. Dennis Saleeby, my graduate social work professor, who required readings about death and dying before it was popular. It was in his class that I developed my first workshop on the subject. That was a major seed.

I am deeply indebted to Dr. Robert Weiss of the Work and Family Research Unit at the University of Massachusetts. Dr. Weiss believed that my papers and brochures would be valuable to families in which a loved one had been killed. Through his inspired paper, *Will It Always Feel This Way?For the Parent Whose Child Has Been Killed,* he confirmed my belief that it is respectable to write from the heart. Dr. Weiss is an inspiration whose influence will continue beyond his years.

I am grateful to Dr. Hannelore Wass, Dr. Camille Wortman, Darrin Lehman, and Dr. Therese Rando for their excellent research and publications that have formed an invaluable cornerstone for my work with victims. I especially thank them for reviewing the book during their busy schedules.

Thanks to Joyce Dace Lombard, Dr. Judy Alexandre, Ron Hillestad, and Dr. Kathleen Wheeler for their helpful text suggestions.

I thank Judge Cathy Stayman Evans for her diligent review

of the criminal justice chapter. Civil attorneys William Shernoff, Charles Lipcon, and Doug Roberts, as well as Fred Beck of Alliance of American Insurers, the late Ralph Jackson of Allstate, and Bob Plunk of Preferred Risk Mutual all deserve appreciation for their consultation regarding financial recovery for victims. David Flowers and Jim Reynolds of Gandy, Michiner, Swindle, Whittaker, Pratt, and Mercer in Fort Worth, Texas were especially helpful, as was financial planner, Jerry Cosby.

While a multitude of victims were remembered and quoted in the book, special thanks go to Janet Barton, Greg Novak, Bob and Pat Preston, Ralph Shelton, Betty Jane Spencer, and Howard Velzey for reading the manuscript and offering constructive criticism.

The second edition was greatly enhanced by the addition of the chapter on suicide. For that, I am grateful for the encouragement and assistance of Anne Seymour. With the assistance of colleague Stephanie Frogge, additions were made to the "Death of a Brother or Sister" chapter in the fourth edition.

This fifth edition adds new findings from the field of trauma grief, an enhanced chapter on spirituality, and a new chapter on the death of a friend or colleague. The chapters on criminal justice and financial issues were updated. The book now includes more quotes from victims of guns. The newly-formed "Bell Campaign" is deeply appreciated for its commitment to stop gun violence, and for its support of this new edition.

Mothers Against Drunk Driving (MADD) made the project possible by allowing me time to write. The national staff, the board of directors, and the MADD chapters have been more than supportive of my work for the past fifteen years. Without that, the book would have been no more than a dream.

Acknowledgements

Finally, I thank my former publisher and editor, Eugene Wheeler, who labored with me as a true colleague, attending victim conferences and speaking with victims to gain a deeper understanding of a victim's experience. His wife, Genie became committed to the project as well and has been a treasured source of support throughout. My new publisher, Bill Mosbrook, supervised this new fifth edition and offered superb guidance. I can't thank enough my friend and colleague Catherine Madigan for her sensitivity as a victim advocate and exquisite skill as a writer and editor. She feels like a gift from God.

I launch *No Time for Goodbyes* fifth edition with the hope that it will touch the hearts and minds of those who feel alone or hopeless. May their grieving and growing be a fitting memorial to the spirits of those whom they have loved.

Janice Harris Lord
March 2000

CONTENTS

PREFACE

Before beginning my work with homicide survivors, I thought I was accustomed to the aftermath of violence. I had worked with children who had been physically and sexually abused. I had counseled battered women. I thought I had witnessed the pinnacle of rage, the depths of despair. I was naive.

When I became Director of Victim Services at the national headquarters of Mothers Against Drunk Driving (MADD), that perspective changed. During the first week of phone calls and letters from victims, I realized that grieving the loss of a loved one who had been killed suddenly, violently, and senselessly is unique.

I met Mary Anna Downing, whose son, Eddie had been killed by a drunk driver just a year and a half before another son, Jimmy was killed in the same manner. I attended Jimmy's funeral and saw him lowered into the ground beside his brother, whose grave was still without grass or tombstone. My mind spun in the awareness that Mary Anna Downing would now have to buy headstones for two children, negotiate with four insurance companies, and be thrust into two separate criminal procedures with a myriad of players. A school cafeteria worker, Mary Anna supplemented her income by selling Avon products. She was now too devastated to work. I wondered how she would survive.

I later met Carl and Mary Mittag. Still grieving the loss of Mary's father to cancer, they now faced the sudden murder of her mother, aunt, and cousin while vacationing in Florida. I witnessed their agony as they attempted to cope not only with their grief, but the frustration brought about by the criminal justice system, wrongful death civil suits, and insurance settlements in

Preface

states far from their home. The criminal trial resulted in a verdict of "not guilty" for the driver, although he was clearly intoxicated. Two years later, the wrongful death suits were still pending and not one cent of insurance money had been paid to the survivors.

As I expanded my attention to other homicide survivors, I met Betty Jane Spencer. Betty Jane's four sons were shot and killed execution-style in their rural Indiana home. Betty Jane was wounded, but survived. As she looks back on the events of that day, she says, "I was killed, too. I just didn't die."

Out of the ashes of Betty Jane's experience, however, she kindled multiple legislative changes for victim's rights in Indiana. She has been a source of strength to many victims who lean on her.

If you comment on her strength, Betty Jane says, "No, I'm not strong. I do have courage though." She attributes her definition of courage to John Wayne: "Courage is being afraid and saddling up anyway."

I have facilitated support groups at which every member present was grieving the death of someone they loved to a violent, senseless act. In these groups, I have witnessed the wonderful healing powers of a stranger _ struggling with his own grief _ who tells another, "I understand something of what you feel. I'm walking in similar shoes."

I am not a victim myself, so my understanding is limited. However, my first-hand work with victims, education, and research over the years has led to a considerable cache of insight that may help homicide survivors to cope.

While I have read and participated in many studies, this book is not intended as a scholarly report on grief research. It will, however, heighten the awareness of professionals seeking to understand more about the experience of a homicide survivor.

This book focuses on the needs of family members and friends of someone who has been killed. It explores the survivor's feelings relative to the degree of trauma they have suffered. It makes practical suggestions for coming to grips with grief and for coping with the systems in which the survivor will be forced to interact.

It is written to help family members and friends of the deceased understand that somehow, someday, with time and effort, they will begin to heal. Recovery will be varied and unique. Each survivor is different. Some homicide survivors may choose to focus on the victim and ignore their own suffering for a time. When they are ready, however, their burden can be lightened. In these pages, they will discover they are not alone.

This book is written in the spirit of a man whose mother, father, wife, and brother were murdered in the Holocaust, and who said:

"... Everything can be taken from a man but one thing: the loss of the human freedoms to choose one's attitude in any given set of circumstances ..."

Viktor Frankl
Man's Search for Meaning[1]

---

1 Frankl, Victor, *Man's Search for Meaning: An Introduction to Logotherapy*, New York: Washington Square Press, 1963 (p. 104).

I

YOUR GRIEF IS UNIQUE

Someone you love has been killed violently, perhaps in a vehicular crash or a freak accident, perhaps murdered. Pain too deep for words may be what you are experiencing now. Or that kind of pain may be a vivid memory.

Death is probably not new to you. You may have previously experienced the death of someone you love. But this is different.

During your lifetime, you may have experienced the death of family members or friends to a terminal illness or old age. Death is rarely easy to accept. However, most human beings recover, and in time, memories of the "good times" replace memories of the sad final days.

The sudden, violent death that took your loved one likely feels unlike anything else that you have experienced. Few, if any, family tragedies are as traumatic as the death of a loved one by homicide or suicide. You may be angrier than you have ever been and sadder than you thought possible. You may have frightening thoughts. You may do strange things. You may be afraid you are "going crazy."

Do not be alarmed. Few people experiencing traumatic grief "go crazy." Getting through your misery can be so devastating, though, that you begin to question your own sanity.

Most people can accept the fact that "accidents" happen. But a sudden accident is more difficult to cope with than an expected death. It is even more traumatic if it came both suddenly and violently. In criminal victimization, those who are left behind have a difficult time grasping that someone chose to be negligent or selected a victim to brutalize. It makes no sense at all.

You may feel further victimized if family members or friends reject you for what happened. Services or programs designed to help you may seem superficial.

Families can never prepare for the violent or sudden death of a loved one. Nor are they prepared to face weeks, months, and even years of waiting until a criminal case is resolved and insurance claims and civil suits are settled. During this time, people who are counted on for support sometimes fail. Unfortunately, many of those who attempt to comfort survivors, and even some professionals who should know better, don't understand that grieving after the traumatic stress of homicide or suicide will be intense and long lasting.

Studies attempting to understand grieving conclude that each person grieves differently. Yet while each person's grief cycle is unique, the studies indicate that victims who suffer similar losses often can understand and share each other's grief journey.

How you grieve depends on a number of things:

- the way you learned to cope with stress in your life before this tragedy;
- the quality of the relationship you had with the person who

was killed;
- the circumstances under which your loved one was killed;
- the success you have dealing with the criminal justice system, insurance companies, and the myriad of other systems you must face in the aftermath of your tragedy;
- your religious beliefs and ethnic customs; and
- the emotional support your family and friends offer while you are grieving.

It is amazing but true that a few people handle trauma well. They seem to bounce back to a fulfilling life soon after their loved one dies. Most of these people have strong support from their family and friends and a substantial supply of good memories about the one who died. Many of these mourners believe their loved one lives on spiritually. However, most families in which someone has been killed have a very difficult time coping.

Anticipated Death

Let us look for a moment at what we know about grief after an anticipated and non-violent death. Doing so will help us understand the unique pain of homicide or suicide. It is tempting to label anticipated and non-violent death as "normal," but few people in grief, even in the best of circumstances, feel "normal." However, the griever who knows ahead of time that death is approaching may react differently than you do.

When people learn that a loved one is likely to die, they may not believe it at first. They may seek several medical opinions to be sure—and rightly so.

As they begin to believe that death really is forthcoming, they may get angry; angry that modern science can develop machines as miraculous as computers, but can't find a cure for particular diseases. They may be angry with God for "allowing" death. They may pray fervently for God to intervene, and then feel frustrated if God doesn't seem to answer their prayers.

They may be sad and depressed as they face the fact that their loved one will die. They may long for relief for their loved one as they see the body deteriorate.

When family members and a loved one are able to accept the reality that death is imminent, they have an opportunity to express their feelings for one another, resolve problems, and relate lovingly and honestly during the last days.

Even in the best of circumstances, though, survivors are often surprised to learn that they will go through many of the same feelings of disbelief, anger, and sadness after the death. It seems to be a part of human nature that emotionally healthy human beings resist death, their own as well as someone else's, and that is probably as it should be.

Approaching death can bring people closer together or it may cause them to distance themselves emotionally. Either way, it is believed to cushion the impact of the death when it comes. Coming to grips with an anticipated death usually takes from three to twenty-four months, according to most research. In some cases it can take years. Most people find that if they "lean in" to grieving, allow their emotions to flow and talk openly about their loss, they will, little by little, be cleansed of much of the pain. Those who attempt to deny their grief and pretend that nothing has happened may have more difficulty.

Traumatic Death

Your experience may be quite unlike what has just been described because death came to your loved one suddenly. You had no time to say "good-bye," "I'm sorry," or "I love you."

The sad part is that she died alone. There were no last "I love

21

you" or "thank you" or "hey, I really appreciate all you do."
There were no soft smiles, no caring words—only screams. Screams
that echoed through the empty chambers of my mind where laughter
once reigned.

> Tammy Luke, written in
> memory of her friend Laura
> Porter

Violence of the Death

The death your loved one faced may have been violent.
Perhaps his or her body was mutilated by a gunshot or a knife
wound. Witnessing the results of a violent death can be extremely
painful for family members or friends of the deceased.

When people are seriously injured, they often undergo
shock and do not immediately experience pain. Those who have
recovered say it was some time before they felt pain, even if they
drifted in and out of consciousness. Most do not remember the
point of impact, whether from an automobile crash, gunshot, or
other form of trauma.

Therefore, the shock to the survivor upon learning of the
tragedy may be more terrifying than that to the person who died.
Even so, you may be thinking that you would have done anything
to prevent your loved one's body from being violated.

Human beings have personalities, and most people believe
they have spirits or souls. But bodies are also important. You grieve
the loss of your loved one's personality and spirit, but you also
may be grieving the loss of his or her living body. You saw it. You
touched it. It touched you. You miss it.

TO MY DEAD DAUGHTER
Fair daughter, sister, friend and heart-mate;
soul's child, Eros, muse and mirror.

I kissed the arching feet,
the small cold hands, the purpled lids.
A drop of blood from your smooth brow
I licked, like any mother beast,
mewing, nuzzling, howling
over its cub.
Mad with pain
I stroke your body _ heavy now _ -
that had such lightness, grace,
its gold warmth now yellowing.
No. This is not you!
You are not here.

I search, my darling, everywhere.
My stunned feet grope forest paths.
Through shared waters my body moves.
I float upon your river of dark hair.
Are you there?
I grasp the air.

Anita Huffington, written in
memory of her daughter

You not only miss the living presence and body of your loved one, but you may deeply resent the fact that the killer did not respect your loved one's body. You may feel guilt that you were unable to protect your loved one, even if you know it was not possible.

Because of the condition of your loved one's body, you may not have been able to view it at the hospital or funeral home. If this was the case, you now rely on fantasies to form a picture of how you think he or she looked.

Chapter 1

You may doubt that your loved one actually died. You may find yourself expecting him or her to walk through the door or call on the telephone at any minute. Most survivors feel this way for awhile, but it may seem more likely if you were unable to spend time with your loved one's body.

Most people who were able to view their loved one are glad they did. If you were unable to do so, you may have to find other ways to assure yourself of the reality of the death.

Michael was so badly battered—many head injuries. I refused to let his three younger brothers go into the hospital room. I regret that now. In an effort to spare them, I robbed them of their last chance to see their brother alive.

Even though the casket was closed to the public, our family did get to see and touch his body before the funeral. His brother James, 15, slipped Mike's graduation key and tassel in his breast pocket before we closed the casket.

Rita Chiavacci,
whose son Michael,
age 19, was killed

Funeral directors are encouraged to allow family members as much choice as possible about viewing the body of a loved one. Most people know what they can handle. If the funeral director describes the condition of the body, survivors can be counted on to make the right choice regarding viewing.

Funeral directors also are encouraged to take photos of the deceased in their final state. Family members who choose not to view the body immediately may wish to look at photographs weeks, months, or years later.

Other options exist for those who did not have an

opportunity to see the body. Photographs of the victim sometimes can be obtained from law enforcement or fire department personnel, the medical examiner, or a representative from the prosecutor's office. These photos can be stark and graphic. Agencies, believing their actions to be compassionate, sometimes are reluctant to allow family members to view them. You may need to be assertive in your request.

Parents of Murdered Children recommends the following procedure for viewing pictures of the deceased: The person wishing to view the photos is encouraged to take their closest support person with them to view the pictures. This is not always a spouse. The person in custody of the photographs is asked to place each picture in a separate envelope, arranging them in order with the least offensive photo on top and the most offensive photo on bottom. The support person is shown the first photograph, then is asked to describe it to the family member or friend. This gives the survivor two sources of data: the description of the photo from the support person and the affect of the support person as he or she views the photo. On that basis, the survivor can make a reasonably informed decision about whether to look at the photograph.

Many times, only one or two photos will be viewed, but the survivor may choose to take copies of the other photos home to view at a later date. They should have that choice if the criminal justice case is complete and there is no longer a legal need for securing the photos within the agency.

Viewing bodies at the scene of the crime is a similar issue. Once emergency medical care has been administered and the crime scene has been properly recorded by the law enforcement agency, survivors should be allowed a choice about seeing, touching, or holding the body of their loved one. Attendants should be very clear in describing the condition of the body so the survivor's choice is an informed one. Again, most people know what they can handle.

Chapter 1

Very rarely does a survivor report regret after being allowed to go to a loved one's body. Most are grateful.

Hospitals have changed policies within the last few years to allow presence and touch through the death experience. Family members should be encouraged to stay as long as they wish with the body of a loved one who has died.

In some cases, a loved one discovers the body before support services arrive. Victims of murder or suicide are frequently found by a family member. Vehicular crashes are sometimes witnessed by family or friends. Shock, numbness, and rage are normal responses to a violent scene. The visual imprint of the death scene can be overwhelming and long lasting.

Professional counselors can help those who are fixated on the death scene to diffuse the impact of the violence. This is accomplished through emotional support as the experience is discussed, and techniques are used to help recall the memory with less horror. With help, positive memories of the loved one will replace distressing images.

Untimeliness of the Death

A sudden death is never timely. Whether the one killed was your child, mate, parent, brother, sister, or friend, the shock can be devastating.

Your Child

If your child was killed, a part of you may feel aborted, too. Your parental drive to nurture and protect remains, but it now has nowhere to go. A child's death feels terribly wrong. You expected to die before your child. It doesn't seem right that this natural pattern was reversed. This is true whether the one killed was a young child or an adult child. Your child is always your child.

"No! You're lying—
It can't be!" I screamed
as I ran about pounding my head.
"I'm sorry," the officer replied,
"but your son didn't make it.
He's dead"
"Oh, dear God, how can it be?"
I cried.
"He was just a kid of seventeen!"

Florence (Mickey) Mikalauskas,
written in memory of her son

Your Mate

If your mate was killed, you may have suddenly lost your best friend, your lover, your co-parent, a breadwinner, and your primary confidant. Being forced to make major decisions alone, to maintain the family, and to grieve, all at the same time, can be devastating.

At 7:30 a.m., my wife died with me at her side. I never saw her conscious. I have nightmares about that moment even still. I feel I let her down. I wish I could have just looked into her eyes once and said, "I love you"

Our second Christmas without Michelle is now approaching. There are no words to explain the grief that I and our three children, Erika, 7, Kimberly, 5, and Jeffrey, 2, have gone through this past year. The two girls still have nightmares. Jeffrey never knew his mother. How can I explain a broken heart and broken dreams?

Joseph Lawrence,
whose 35-year-old wife was
killed

Chapter 1

Your Parent

If your parent was killed, no matter how old he or she was, you may deeply regret that the death was undignified. Some people may say, "He lived a good, full life," but you may feel guilty about never having said, "thank you for giving me life," or "goodbye," or "I'm sorry that your death came violently."

> *February 11, 1982, was a very long day*
> *——the longest. My mother's surprise*
> *visit turned into tragedy. Now two*
> *days later, eyes red, I'm sitting on*
> *an airplane flying my mother's body home.*
> *How do you say to your brothers, "Mom is*
> *dead—killed in a needless crash?"*

> *I had a rough year and, as always, Mom*
> *was coming to comfort me. Now, this is Mom's*
> *last flight home to Iowa. It was so quick—*
> *so unnecessary—I miss her so much I can*
> *hardly bear it.*

> *Barbara Brodt*

Your Sibling

If your brother or sister was killed, you may feel guilt about being alive, even though you know this is irrational. Siblings are often alike. A sibling's death can remind you of your own mortality, making it especially difficult to face. If your brother or sister could be killed in an instant, so could you. The pain to the family after a sibling has died may leave you believing the wrong child died.

> *Dale, I'm just so glad for the time we had together. And I'm glad we were close. But I'm so sad and so sorry we won't have any more laughter or good times together. I will always love you and I will never, ever stop missing*

you. I just pray that no other brother or sister will have to feel the way I feel now. There is an empty space inside of me that can't ever be filled again. No one can take your place.

Debra Mumblo,
whose brother was killed

Your Friend or Colleague

If your friend or colleague was killed, you may feel like your brother or sister was the victim. In this fast-paced, mobile society, relatives may be geographically remote or emotionally distant. Friends and colleagues can feel closer than family.

That *my wonderful young friend could be gunned down within an instant shattered me. I knew I had to open my arms to his family, but at the same time, I desperately needed people to see me as a legitimate mourner also.*

Kimberly Rowland,
whose friend was
murdered with a gun

Senselessness of the Death

Another difficult component of grieving the death of your loved one is the senselessness of the act. You may be able to understand when bodies wear out with age or when diseases cannot be cured. But violent deaths are intentional or a result of negligence. Someone is at fault.

Murder is the brutal, purposeful assault of an unwilling victim. Suicide differs only in that the victim was willing.

Sometimes, murderers have been previously incarcerated in prison or a mental hospital. If they had remained there, you believe, the death may have been avoided. You do not understand why society failed to protect your loved one from this killer.

Most vehicular crashes are caused by someone who chose to be irresponsible. About half are caused by drunk drivers. Most involve speeding. Many are caused by people who refuse to stop and rest, and then fall asleep behind the wheel. Most crashes could have been prevented.

One of the most difficult losses for survivors is a murder in which the offender was known: the baby-sitter who kills a child, the teenager who kills his date, the jealous lover who kills the "ex," the drunk driver who kills one of his own family members.

If you know the offender, your mind may be in turmoil with confusing and conflicting feelings. You may feel guilty because you didn't intervene sooner. It is difficult to blame someone you know. You may worry about what will happen to the offender in the criminal and civil justice systems. Knowing that your loved one's death could have been prevented may be one of the most painful aspects of your grieving.

Criminal Justice Frustrations

Most violent deaths result in the survivors's involvement with the criminal justice system. This can be a difficult and frustrating experience as you face procedures you do not understand. You may not understand why the State requires an autopsy. An autopsy is performed to determine the exact cause of death, which will become a component of the criminal trial. An autopsy following a suicide rules out homicide as the cause of death. You may be left out of meetings and hearings that you believe you have a right to attend. Unless you are assertive, you may be left out of decisions at critical stages of the criminal case.

I contacted the District Attorney's office about two months after my children were killed. I was given the impression that my presence and questions were an imposition to the Assistant DA handling the case. To me, my children were human beings—not just reports lying on someone's desk.

Was it wrong for me, their mother, to want to see that the man who had killed my children was prosecuted?

I was not told when the trial would be held and found out only when it appeared in the newspaper. I wasn't allowed to be in the courtroom because my "presence" might bias the jury. Yet the offender was present through the entire trial. The jury never even saw pictures of my beautiful children—and they never knew who I was as I sat alone in the hall the three days of the trial.

Mary Mitchell,
whose children, Bart, 5,
and Gayla, 7, were killed

Financial Stress

Your financial security may be threatened after the violent and sudden death of a loved one. Emergency medical care and funerals are costly. You may have missed several days or weeks of work. You may have difficulty concentrating when you return to work. That may threaten your job security. You may have hired a special investigator to ensure ample evidence for prosecution and a civil suit. You may have paid for the travel of relatives to come to the funeral. All of that takes money.

Faith/Philosophy of Life Issues

Even if you haven't thought much about "life," "death," or "God" before, you may be thinking about these things now. On the other hand, you may have previously thought a lot about these topics and thought you had them all figured out. Now you may find that none of your ideas work under these new circumstances. This sense of alienation can cause you despair. It will take time and effort to reconstruct your basic beliefs to accommodate this tragedy.

Chapter 1

Summary

I have not painted a pretty picture. You knew your experience was far from "pretty" when you opened this book. Your loss was sudden and unanticipated. It was violent. It was senseless and unnecessary. It was untimely. It may have plunged you into a criminal justice system that is complex and cold. You may suddenly find you are under financial stress. And you may be struggling to develop a faith or philosophy that works in the face of this unimaginable, inexcusable act.

It is not the purpose of this book to bewilder you or perplex you. Its purpose is to help you understand why this grief reaction is not like others you have experienced. It is to help you understand why you feel angry when others tell you that you should "get on with your life."

Don't be alarmed if you cry while reading this book. That only means that you need to cry. Grieving and mourning involve crying. It is painful, but it is healthy. Most people feel some release from pain after crying because it helps them get in touch with parts of themselves they couldn't touch in any other way.

Understanding more about the unique aspects of your traumatic grief will not change how you feel about your loved one, but it may enable you to feel more comfortable with yourself. It may enable you, also, to take what others say with a grain of salt if their expectations do not fit your own experience.

II

GRIEF and MOURNING FOLLOWING TRAUMA

We are all vulnerable to deep emotional reactions after a traumatic experience. These reactions are normal responses to abnormal events.

The kind of person you were before your loved one was killed will determine how you react and recover after a tragic event. If you are physically and emotionally healthy, had a good relationship with your loved one, have a supportive network of friends, feel basically in control of your life, and tend to view a crisis as a challenge rather than a catastrophe, you may recover more quickly.

No matter how "together" you are, however, recovering from a traumatic and unexpected death will require patience and work. You will never be exactly the same again, so don't expect recovery to be complete.

Getting better means:

- solving problems and completing tasks in your daily work routine again,

- sleeping well and having energy again,

- feeling good enough about yourself to be hopeful about your present and your future,

- being able to enjoy the pleasurable and beautiful things in life.

You probably will be able to achieve these in time. For most people it takes months, even years. Current research indicates bereavement following a sudden, violent death is intense for three to four years and is never complete.

Some people worry that they will forget their loved one if they "get better." Stop worrying. You will never forget. You will always cherish the memory of your loved one. You will always be sorry you didn't share life with him or her for many more years. In time, however, you will remember the happy times more frequently than the painful ones that fill your mind now.

Stage Theories

People have been writing about "stages" as long as they have been talking about death and crime victimization, including the sudden death of homicide. Most of us know about Elizabeth Kubler-Ross' stages: denial, anger, bargaining, depression, and acceptance. Her research was based primarily on children and who were facing death in the near future, and their parents. Marton Bard and Dawn Sangrey are early pioneers in research about crime victimization. They refer to the stages of initial disorganization/ shock, struggle/recoil, and readjustment. Dr. Therese Rando, one of our country's finest contemporary grief researchers, speaks of three stages: avoidance, confrontation, and re-establishment.

Stages of grief can help us to understand the grieving process, but we must remember that stages are not firm, concrete, and predictable. They suggest trends that may help you to feel more normal as you read about them. But they are descriptive, not prescriptive. They become prescriptive when you start to believe that you are not "grieving properly" if you do not fit into a stage sequence. Over-emphasis on stages overlooks the totality of life. You approach your trauma as a unique individual, different from someone else in some other town who experienced a similar trauma. Your daily life differs. A "stage" may vary by month or by hour, and it can be affected by who you are with at any given time.

Be gentle and patient with yourself as you proceed during various stages of grief. If you reach out to help someone else at a later date, remember that it is harmful to try to push people from one stage to another. It's easy to think that "denial" or "shock" represent character weakness and that people should "face what happened."

Components of Response to Sudden Death

The following components are not "stages." They are pieces of the grief experience that most survivors experience from time to time over the course of their grief.

Denial/Shock/Numbness

Denial is a wonderful thing. It is nature's way of warding off the full impact of trauma until a person is ready to absorb the totality of the shock. Most people, upon being told that a loved one has been killed, are rendered too weak to undertake the overwhelming task of grieving.

You may have gone into shock after hearing about the unexpected death of a loved one. Shock is similar to being given a general anesthetic. With the help of a quick spurt of adrenalin, endorphins, opiods, and other chemicals, your initial response may have been "fight," "flight," or "freeze." Police officers who deliver death notifications say it is not uncommon for "fighters" to physically attack a person who has delivered the bad news. Those whose reaction is "flight" may faint or run to escape the pain. "Frozen fright" describes those unable to react.

It was 12:30 am on June 10th when the call came from the hospital telling me that my son, John had been injured. Because I was alone, the police came to pick me up. All the way to Massachusetts General, the two officers in front talked about trivial matters. Neither of them spoke a word to me. When we got to the hospital, I was questioned about insurance and then put in a room by myself.

I sat alone reciting the Hail Mary aloud to break the silence and tension. Eventually, a young doctor, obviously tired and aggravated, entered the room, hopped up on a gurney, and said, "Your son has expired." That's all.
"I don't know what to say," I stammered, as if I could ever be prepared for such an event. I ran from the hospital, and outside, screamed, and screamed, and screamed.

> *Margaret Grogan, whose son, John was stabbed in the heart at a graduation party*

I prayed all the way to the hospital, "Please God, at least give him five more minutes." But it was too late. Since I'm a registered nurse, I've had to tell people that their child was dead. It's something that you never get used to. But I never dreamed I would walk into an emergency room and have my husband tell me, "Oh God, Sally, our baby is dead." I watched a nice man dissolve before my eyes. I felt my 15 year-old son hitting on me, begging me to say his brother wasn't dead. I watched my daughter crumble and say, "Mom, I want to get the guy who did this"

Grief After Trauma

Sally Jeanes, whose 18-year-old son, Jason was killed by a drunk driver

Regardless of the initial impact, if you are like most people, you soon find yourself in a state of numbness. Looking back on it now, you may wonder how you remained calm. You may have completed some tasks that now seem impossible. You probably have a hard time remembering exactly what you did during those first few days.

I was having trouble making sense of it and nurses were staring at me. I didn't want to think about the boys and what had happened to them. I was alive. Maybe they were, too. Words seemed to hang in the air while I tried to make sense of them. Words like "dead" and "autopsy" floated through. I didn't want to hear them. But all I could say was, "Please don't tell me how many are dead

Betty Jane Spencer, recalling her condition before being told that her four sons had been killed

During this time, people may have commented on how "strong" you were. One of the saddest parts of trauma is that people assume you are strong when you are in shock. You may appear strong, but you feel like a mechanical robot. When the shock wears off and you desperately need your friends, they have resumed life as usual, believing that you are doing fine.

For the first few months I was in a daze. I was plagued by flashbacks, but I only half believed it was real. Friends commented on how brave and calm and strong I was. What they did

37

*not know was that I had not yet fully comprehended the enormity
of what had happened.*

> *Barbara Kaplan, who was seriously
> injured, but survived a shooting in
> which two of her friends were killed*

Denial following a violent and unanticipated loss should be considered normal and functional. You should travel through this part of grief at your own pace. Denial will serve you well until you are stronger and better able to cope. It is impossible to push through any part of grieving in order to "get it over with." If you cannot think clearly, seem forgetful, and seem detached, be patient with yourself. If you need help, ask for it. However, be very careful about using alcohol and sedating prescriptive drugs. They will push you into an unnatural denial. Allow your own body to compensate for the trauma.

Fear/Vulnerability

Many survivors are surprised to find that they feel anxious, fearful, and powerless in the aftermath of a killing. Although you know that tragedies occur, you may have believed that they happened to other people. Before your trauma, you may have felt uniquely invulnerable. It wouldn't happen to you.

After your loved one was killed, you may have felt that life was "out of kilter." It's strange how we tend to believe that good things happen to good people and bad things happen to bad people. That belief, for you, is now proven false.

You may feel that you and your remaining loved ones are more vulnerable than others. That's frightening. You will need to think rationally and work hard to risk going out even when it frightens you. Little by little, you can overcome these fears. It is maddening to realize that the killer not only destroyed your loved one, but also damaged the part of you that was previously confident and carefree.

The fact that I could be killed hit me with full force. I felt powerless and off-balance. Would I feel frightened of everyone I didn't know?.... I saw each stranger as a potential killer. I envied those who walked trusting others. I worried about becoming weak and fearful.

                           Jean Goldberg

If you think about it, everything we do in life depends on others acting in a rational and predictable way. When you get in a car and drive it away, you're investing a lot of trust in every other driver on the road. So what happens when that trust is gone? Try driving down a two-lane highway with cars passing you just a few feet over in the oncoming lane. Your guts will be in knots if you can handle it at all. When you start to see every faceless stranger as a potential madman or thug, you're not only scared, but depressed. You really feel betrayed!

                           Barbara Kaplan

Since that week I feel differently about life. I don't feel so young. I'm 27, but after losing my 4-year-old son, I know there's nothing fair about death. I often think it could happen again. I think of death often. I told my mother the other day that I'll miss her when she dies.

                           Kim Keyes, whose child, Kurt, was killed in an auto mobile crash along with three other relatives and a family friend

The fear and vulnerability of knowing that tragedy can strike anyone at anytime has an almost existential quality. It leads to questions like, "What is life, anyhow?" "What are we here for?" "Why do people have to die?" "Why didn't God do something to stop it?" These issues can be doubly overwhelming to adolescents who are just beginning to try to figure out life, let alone death. Facing the pain in the household can be so overwhelming that young people may seek ways to escape rather than face their own vulnerability.

Physical Symptoms

Stress following trauma can make you physically sick. As you experience sadness, confusion, fear, anxiety, and anger, you may find that you have no appetite. You may feel weak, as if you couldn't take another step. You may feel exhausted, but when you go to bed you can't sleep or you sleep only a short time. Your sex drive may be gone or diminished.

Many survivors speak of pain, including stomachaches and a heaviness in the chest, a symptom some refer to as "a broken heart." You may feel nervous and edgy.

Some survivors begin to think about suicide as these symptoms escalate. They wish they could die, too, to escape the pain. Friends and relatives who care are critical to your well-being at these times.

You may need help in thinking rationally about what is best for you and your family.

You may need to see a doctor, especially if you are not eating or sleeping. The immune system of most people in grief loses some of its effectiveness. This may cause you to be more vulnerable to disease.

People in grief may also be accident-prone. Many become involved in automobile accidents, falls, or other mishaps. These can happen because you are preoccupied with your loss.

If you are vulnerable to cardiovascular disease or other serious illnesses, you must have regular checkups. Some research has suggested a correlation between grief and the onset of cancer If you use tobacco or drugs, including alcohol, you will need to very carefully monitor your use. Some grieving people increase their usage in order to escape and to sleep. This leads to more problems that are serious. Alcohol is a depressant. It will increase rather than decrease your grief. It will also aggravate other physical conditions. Grieving, as painful as it is, is usually best leaned into and fully experienced. Alcohol and other drugs will not help. They may prolong your grief.

Your doctor may prescribe medication to help you eat or sleep during the initial phase of grieving. Do not consider this a weakness. You have suffered severe trauma and deserve professional help to begin feeling better. You will probably need the help of prescribed drugs for a short time only. Even if you don't want to feel better yet, you owe it to yourself and your family to stay in good health.

Anger

You may be surprised at the intensity of anger you feel for the person who killed your loved one. The more senseless the act, the more angry you may feel. Some survivors do not feel angry, but most do, even to the point of rage.

I didn't think it was possible to hate someone so much. I felt the most deep penetrating hate I have ever known in my life. I'm a pastor and it's pretty shocking to find out the kinds of feelings one can have.

> *Tinka Bloedow, whose 14 year-old daughter, Tee Ja, was killed by a drunk driver*

You may wish desperately that the person who killed your loved one would show some remorse or say "I'm sorry." That probably won't happen.

Many offenders do not feel remorse. Some are indeed sorry. Their attorneys, however, will warn them to make no contact with you because such contact can be considered an admission of guilt.

Some people experience anger in the early stages of grieving, others feel angry later after some of the numbness has worn off. You may have been angry before you were willing to admit it.

It is unfortunate that most of us were taught as children that some feelings are bad. Most of us heard:
- "You shouldn't get angry."
- "It's wrong to feel jealous."
- "It's sinful to feel vengeance."
- "Rage is a terrible thing."

Feelings are not right or wrong. They simply are. Your behavior may be good or bad, right or wrong, appropriate or not appropriate. Your thinking may be clear or foggy, rational or irrational.

But your feelings are simply your feelings with no "shoulds" attached. It is silly of people to suggest that you should stop having a particular feeling. It is impossible.

It might comfort victims, especially those who feel cheated by the criminal justice system, to know that it is acceptable and helpful to fantasize about the "justice" they would impose on the killer.

One of the most helpful things I learned in coping was that feelings are involuntary, like the urge to sneeze, and can seldom be suppressed. Even the most negative of angry thoughts and feelings are not wrong. "Wrong" comes in only if they translate into behaviors.

> *Janet Barton, whose son was murdered*

It is very important that you not act destructively in response to your feelings of anger. You must force yourself to think rationally about what you will do with your anger. But what you feel is what you feel.

You may find that you are not only angry with the person who killed your loved one, but many others, including God, the doctors, investigating officers, and even your family. You may be angry with everyone who seems to be going on with life as if nothing happened. You may even be angry at your dead loved one for abandoning you, no matter how much you know it wasn't his or her fault. Obviously, such anger is misplaced, and should not be acted out.

And there is anger. My anger didn't stop at God or at the murderers. I hated everything and everyone. It was a raw, ugly, destructive feeling that could rise in me and control me for days on end.

> *Betty Jane Spencer,*

whose four sons were
murdered by gun

The injustice of your loved one's death, the deep hurt you feel, and the loss of future dreams may all add up to rage, a wordless drive to do something. Most of the things you think about doing, however, must remain as thoughts. Try not to act out on your rage.

I fantasized for a year about going into the courtroom and blowing his head off. But I decided to leave it all in God's hands. Things have a way of turning out.

June Sanborn, whose only child Diane, was murdered by choking, stabbing, and sexual mutilation

It's okay to think about it, and it's very helpful to talk about it with someone who is willing to listen. If you can find someone who has felt the same way with whom to share your feelings, you are very fortunate.

Sadly, many friends will not be willing to listen as you ventilate some intense feelings. Their response may make you more angry. It would be helpful if others could understand that expressing intense feelings means you are taking responsibility for your thoughts and are not likely to act on them.

Allowing yourself to express the feelings will probably free your mind, enabling you to be more open and realistic in your thinking and planning for the future.

Anger manifests itself physically as well as emotionally. If you suppress anger, or try to prevent yourself from feeling it, you may develop problems in your body. Symptoms can include headaches, stomachaches, colitis, backaches, high blood pressure, and others.

On the other hand, doing something physical often helps. Some people run, exercise vigorously, or clean house. Others keep a journal, or write letters to the offender (which is usually best unmailed). Some cry, yell, and scream.

What you do with your anger really doesn't matter as long as you admit that it's there and you don't hurt yourself or anyone else when expressing it.

You may find that your anger is serving a somewhat useful purpose. Deep sadness may be lurking beneath the anger. While anger does not feel good, it is usually less painful than sadness. Anger can either be focused on someone else or it can be directed in a wide spectrum, not seeming to attach to anyone or anything for long. Sadness is focused inside yourself. You will eventually need to give up some of the anger, rage, and vengeance to experience the feelings underneath.

When you decide to discover what's beneath the anger, you may find gut-wrenching agony. By being willing to face it, you may find some relief from your anger. You may think that you owe it to your loved one to remain angry. That doesn't make a lot of sense. But what you do with your anger and when you decide to look beneath it are up to you.

This somewhat confused society of ours seems to be telling us in print, on television, and in the movies that anger must be ventilated at all cost. Research is not finding that to be so. In fact, those who spend much of their lives spewing anger are those who are more likely than others to get sick. The goal is to get what you want, not just to ventilate.

As someone recently said, "If blowing your stack pollutes the air, you're not going to win!"

You may hear that the prosecutor is contemplating a plea bargain, which you do not understand, and that he has no plan to consult you. That may be enough to enrage you! But ask yourself, "How can I get what I want?" Throwing a fit in the prosecutor's office or writing a nasty "letter to the editor" is more likely to alienate than to get what you want.

Call the prosecutor and ask for a fifteen-minute appointment to discuss the case. Calmly ask why he is considering the plea rather than pushing for the original charges. Sometimes there is a very good reason. In several states, second-degree murder is being charged in serious drunk driving death cases. The legal elements required to accomplish a second-degree murder conviction are complex. Perhaps, as the investigation is carried out, not all the necessary elements can be proven. In such a case, it might be better to accept a guilty plea to a lesser offense than to risk losing everything. If it's a judgement call, you may want to proceed to trial. You may be willing to risk losing the case in order to risk winning. Many prosecutors will take your wishes into consideration, but they retain ultimate discretion in the decision. Some will not because they do not want to risk acquittals on their record. In any event, you may feel a sense of relief if you discuss your concerns with the prosecutor.

Post-Traumatic Stress/Guilt

For a long time, it was believed that most of the painful stress people feel comes from within. Depressed people were thought to have serious internal conflicts, which needed to be worked out.

Now, we understand that external trauma is also a valid

basis for continuing distress. While this understanding may or may not help you feel better, it is good news. It is good news because it means that you are not "crazy" just because you are experiencing very painful symptoms as a result of your loved one's death.

As denial and shock wear off, you may experience some feelings that are foreign and frightening. You may find that particular memories of the trauma keep intruding into your mind. They may be particular sights or sounds. You may have repeated nightmares. Something may make you feel as if the trauma is happening again. If you are aware of what the trigger is _ perhaps the scene of the death, a certain song, certain events _ you may almost compulsively avoid the trigger, somewhat like a phobia.

You may feel that the external world doesn't have much meaning anymore. You may feel like withdrawing because it seems that no one understands your pain. You may have difficulty concentrating, feeling absent-minded and confused.

THE MOTHER LODE

A single eye blazing in my forehead,
I mine your death.
Sifting through the layers,
hording every glint.

Here,
a pile of undone dreams.
And here,
a mound of guilt, if onlys,
blasted touch.
My fossil love.

Blackened with loss,

Chapter 2
deeper and deeper
I dig
for the mother lode.

Anita Huffington,
written in memory
of her daughter

You may struggle with guilt. "If only I had _____,"
becomes a familiar theme for nearly all family members of a
homicide or suicide.

Human beings tend to believe a lot of things that don't
make sense when examined closely. For instance:

- People who love each other should always be responsible for
  each other and be able to protect each other.
- If I had been a better person, this wouldn't have happened to
  my loved one.
- If I begin to feel better it will mean that I didn't love him/her
  enough.
- It is not right that my loved one died and I continue to live.

You may find that when you cry, beneath the tears are the words,
"I'm sorry, I'm sorry, I'm sorry."

Perhaps you feel guilty because you still believe the old
adage, "Good things happen to good people and bad things happen
to bad people." It may seem that if you can just find a way to
prove that you were guilty (bad), at least you can hang on to an
old belief which makes some sense of your loved one's death.

Perhaps the most difficult part of grieving is to look
rationally at why your beliefs make you feel guilty. You may,
indeed, be responsible for some component of your loved one's
death. If so, acknowledge it and see if you can find a way to
forgive yourself. If you made a bad judgement, you probably

made the best one you knew how to make at the time. Try not to exaggerate your role because that will confuse you.

In most cases, other factors were largely responsible for your loved one's death. The person who killed your loved one either chose to do so or was negligent in such a way that the death happened, although it was not intentional. Forces of nature also play a role. One law of nature is that when two powerful opposing forces collide, one or both are destroyed. It would be nice, maybe, if such laws did not always work. On the other hand, it would be frightening to live in a world where nature's laws sometimes worked and sometimes didn't.

You may conclude, by thinking rationally, that you were 5% responsible and someone else was 95% responsible. In that case, take on only 5% of the guilt, not 100%.

Talking with others who truly understand what you're going through can help you look at your guilt realistically. It will be hard work for them and for you.

Feeling less guilty won't take away your sadness or your anger, but it can be a big load off our shoulders. It will be worth the effort to lesson your burden.

Acknowledgment/Accommodation

The word "acceptance" is not used here because the sudden, violent killing of someone you love is never "acceptable." In the beginning, some people believe they will never be happy again. They go through a period of time when they aren't ready to feel better. Others are eager to feel better and work to find ways to do it.

Whether you are ready to feel better or not, you might

want to look to others who have survived the ordeal and have managed to regain strength and find happiness again. They can be encouraging models.

It is a fact that your life will never be the same as it was before your loved one was killed. But it probably will be a lot better than it is now as you read this book.

Acknowledging what happened means believing that it happened as it did, based on all you have learned. It means you no longer have to pretend it did not happen in the manner it did. It means being willing to face and experience the pain rather than avoiding it by over-activism or escape into alcohol or other drugs. It means deciding how to live with your memories. Memories can never be taken from you even though other people may tell you you should move on. Your greater fear is probably forgetting some things you don't want to forget. Many people find it helpful to write down six to ten especially wonderful memories. Get them out and read them often. You may want to save other mementos with your writings, such as a lock of hair, perfume, aftershave, or pieces of clothing. Use these from time to time to cherish the memory. Remind yourself of the good memories when you feel yourself slipping into pain again.

Accommodation comes when you decide you care whether your own life continues or not. I will never forget Trey, and I will look forward to seeing him in Heaven, but I am going on with my life here, and I find joy in it.

Ralph Shelton, whose son was shot and killed by a sniper

Sorrow

You will always feel sorrow that your loved one died tragically and that the long relationship you might have enjoyed was cut short. But the sorrow is different than the height, width and depth of trauma that most survivors experience for the first few months or years after loss. Its parameters are not clear.

Some people describe the sorrow as a "misty fog on life," of which they are not always aware. They simply realize that life is not quite as bright, not quite as light as it was before. Values change. You may be impatient with trivia. You may feel misunderstood. But a sense of sorrow is not the same as being overwhelmed with grief.

Every time I tell our story, I feel cleansed when it is finished. It's important that people know what a neat kid Kurt was. For the first months, we dwelled on things we didn't do with Kurt. Now we think of things we did do. It's more positive. You need to celebrate what their lives meant to you.

Kim Keyes, whose 4-year-old son, Kurt, was killed by a drunk driver

Grief Spasms

It is likely that you will experience sudden grief spasms from time to time over the years. Survivors are often surprised to find that even in the midst of a series of good days, something may bring on a spasm of grief. Anniversaries often are difficult; the birthday of the loved one, the anniversary of the death, the wedding anniversary, Mother's Day, Father's Day. Holidays in which family togetherness is a tradition are often very difficult for families experiencing sudden loss. Certain songs can cause a grief spasm. Seeing someone who resembles your loved one can bring on a grief spasm.

Strange as it may seem, though, grief spasms can be understood as celebrations: celebrations of a relationship that meant so much to you that episodes of grief can still overcome you.

Nearly all survivors are able to say that they would rather have known their loved one as long as they did than not at all. Being able to experience the depth of sadness and the height of joy is to be fully alive, fully human. Most people are glad they are capable of having strong feelings. Experiencing the strong feelings means that shock symptoms and numbness are no longer necessary and the fullness of the experience of the trauma can be absorbed.

As time goes by, grief spasms will come less frequently and less intensely. Most survivors are able to acknowledge that their loved one would want it that way.

Your loved one would want to be fondly remembered from time to time, and even missed. But if you remain caught up in a chronic sense of desperation, the possibility of more set backs could evolve. That would benefit no one and would not be the wish of your loved one.

On some days I'm fine. Then something will happen and I will be right back where I was. I don't cry as much as I did in the beginning. But I don't laugh as much as I did before the crash. Part of me will never come back. But I want it to come back.

> *Sally Jeanes, whose*
> *18-year-old son, Jason, was*
> *killed*

Focus on Life

Another component of acknowledgment or "getting better" is an increasing focus on life and a decreasing focus on death. Early on, you may have felt that you barely existed. Others who told you to cheer up and get on with your life may have seemed unwilling to share your grief journey. They may have been uncomfortable around you.

You may be disappointed with family and friends for their lack of sensitivity and understanding. It can make you frustrated and angry. However, you will have to decide for yourself when it is right to give more of your attention to living. You can use your grief to continue to drag you down or you can use it to rebuild your life, probably with more compassion and understanding than you had before.

You don't have to remain a victim. It's your choice. One day, I realized I could focus on the fact that I was surviving rather than on how much I was diminished by Adrianne's murder. I was getting up in the morning and going to bed at night. I felt I was living, no longer controlled by the tragedy.

Linda Jones, whose daughter was shot and killed

By having experienced trauma, you eventually will be able to keep life in perspective better than other people. Some survivors seem to develop a peace and inner wisdom that others lack.

I feel almost invincible. I have survived the worst thing that could ever happen. All other problems pale in comparison. If I could survive that, I can survive anything.

Ralph Shelton, whose son was shot and killed by a sniper

Chapter 2

Call to Justice

In some cases, enduring trauma ignites a spark of activity to right some of the wrongs involved in a sudden violent death. Most survivors want to prevent it for others.

Thousands of men, women, and teenagers have joined Mothers Against Drunk Driving after the death of a loved one at the hands of a drunk driver. Their desire is to help other injured victims and survivors cope emotionally, help them through the criminal justice system, and to prevent drunken driving crashes.

After their daughter, Lisa was killed; Charlotte and Bob Hullinger founded Parents of Murdered Children as a support for other families forced to endure such tragedy.

The Compassionate Friends has more than 600 groups around the country where parents of children who have died comfort each other.

Rabbi Harold Kushner wrote *When Bad Things Happen to Good People* after his son died. He has continued to write other books that have been helpful to others in difficult situations.

The Bell Campaign was organized in 1999 by victims of guns to prevent gun death and injury, and to support victims of gun trauma.

Not all survivors will choose to undertake such large and noble tasks by reaching out to others. But most are willing, even eager, to touch others who are surviving the loss of a loved one to a violent death. By doing so, they offer one of the most treasured gifts a human being can give to another.

Suggestions

- Understand that the shock and injustice of losing someone you love to a sudden, violent, and senseless death can result in grief with a wider range and depth of feelings. Your grief may last longer than that for survivors of anticipated, non-violent death. If you are coping well, wonderful! But if you are having a hard time, be patient with yourself. Many people struggle for months and years before they feel a resolution of their grieving.

- Maintain regular contact with your physician for several years to be sure that you do not acquire a stress-related physical condition.

- Try to delay major decisions, such as moving, remarrying, deciding to have a baby, or changing jobs for at least one year. No matter how positive they seem, major decisions will create additional stress.

- Feel your feelings, whether they are sadness, rage, or vengeance. Find a way to express them, perhaps through writing, sharing with someone else, or through physical activity. Try to think rationally and to act responsibly.

- Take a realistic look at any guilt you feel. If you are guilty in part for what happened, try to forgive yourself. If God can, can't you? Do not carry a load of guilt that is not applicable to you.

- Try to understand family members who may be grieving differently. It is rare for any two people in a family to handle trauma the same way. Remember that there are no rules for how one should grieve. Try to talk about what you are feeling and encourage others to do the same. Attempt to receive what you hear, even though your experience may be different.

- Be patient with others who say inept things to you. Very rarely are such comments made to hurt you. While most people desperately want to help you, they may not know what to say or do. Try to be grateful for their attempt, if not the end result.

- Remember that no one can fill the shoes of the loved one who has been killed. It is unrealistic to think that another person or activities can fill the vacuum now in your heart. Expecting another person to fulfill you places a terrible burden on him or her.

- Seek the support and understanding of others who have gone through similar trauma. You and your family can benefit from the assistance of others. Call your local Mental Health Association, hospice, and/or clergy to locate support groups and professional counselors who understand the grief that follows your unique loss and trauma. You do not have to handle this alone.

- Find a way to make a positive contribution from your tragedy. This does not mean imposing your memories or experience on others. It means making yourself available to them on their terms. Affiliating with action-oriented organizations is one way to reach out to others.

- Realize that getting better does not mean that you didn't love your loved one enough. Nor does it mean that you will forget him or her. When and how you begin to feel better and what your pilgrimage toward recovery is like, are up to you.

III

DEATH of a DAUGHTER or SON

Mother and Father as Parents

If you are a parent, you probably spent much of your time thinking about how to protect your children, nurture them into adulthood, and then "let go."

When parenting is successful, you expect your children to continue to love you as they become adults. You do not expect them to remain dependent on you. In fact, as you become older, you may depend on them to care for you. And in time, you expect to die and be survived by your children. When your child dies, every one of those expectations is aborted.

The way you nurture a child is different from the way you care for a mate, parents, or friends. When your child is very young, he is totally dependent on you. One amazing thing about human nature is that nurturing a baby, toddler, or a young child is as fulfilling for the parent as it is for the child. That is true, however, only if the parent is emotionally healthy. Emotionally inadequate parents sometimes abuse or neglect their children.

If you are a healthy parent, you are so bonded to your young child that comforting him and keeping him content also makes you comfortable and content. The emptiness that remains when you no longer have your child to nurture can be so painful that some have referred to it as a chronic ache.

Chapter 3

This space is within me all the time it seems. Sometimes the empty space is so real I can almost touch it. I can almost see it. It gets so big sometimes I can't see anything else.

Mary Sennewald

As children grow older, they develop a sense of themselves that is separate from their parents. This need to separate is a normal part of child development. New behaviors during this stage often require parents to discipline the child. Parents may feel an increased need to protect their child as they see him or her grow up.

All children make mistakes. It is hard for a parent to decide when to step in and protect the child, and when to let the child learn by experiencing the consequences of his mistakes.

Parents are strongly driven, however, to protect their child from serious harm no matter how old the child. If they had the choice, most parents would rather die themselves than have their child seriously hurt or killed.

A difficult part of grieving for parents whose child has been killed is the fact that they were not able to protect their child. They may feel extremely angry with themselves for not preventing the tragedy. They may feel guilty, as if the child's death was their fault, even if they know it was not.

All day long I listen for his step,
his whistle, his sweet, uncertain song.
I listen until the silence tightens
round my throat.

Oh God, you know I'd give my life
to hear his voice again.

58

To feel, once more, the touch of his
young, eager hand.
To stand and watch him play,
And feel the pride leap in me like a flame.

I'd give my life, I say_ and yet
I wouldn't. I must stay here and
do my job until I've earned the right to go away.

Elsie Robinson

Coping with the death of an older child is different from coping with the death of a young child. Parents may love them no more or less, but their life experience with them is different. As children become older, they take more risks, check out more unknown territory, and try to solve their own problems. All of that is a very normal part of adolescent development. These phrases will probably have a familiar ring to parents of teenagers.

"I've got to be me!"

"You have got to let me grow up!"

"Get off my back. Weren't you ever a teenager?"

You may recall your child stomping out of the room or slamming doors. Parents are usually resistant to these kinds of words and behaviors. That, too, is normal. While the push and pull of raising a teenager is not always pleasant, it is a sign that the teen is looking for and finding his own values. That is good.

When an older child is killed, parents may have a very difficult time realizing that they were doing the right thing by allowing their child to take risks. If you chose to allow your child some freedom, and it resulted in your child's death, it will not help to place all the blame on yourself. You probably made the best decision you knew how to make at the time.

> *So many recollections bring you to me-*
> *Your insistence on being just you-*
> *"Stubborn," we said.*
> *But no, you were "right.."*
> *You knew what you wanted since age two.*

> *Friends, problems, college life, romance from afar,*
> *Sorority joys, world troubles, future dreams*
> *"Mom, don't expect grandkids or even marriage for awhile...*
> *....maybe never"*

> *You prepared me it seems.*

> *Thank you, Valerie, for being our daughter.*
> *Your mother and dad love you so.*
> *We didn't tell you that very often.*
> *So now our tears must let you know.*

Katherine D. Guayante,
in memory of Valerie

Another component of grieving when a child has been killed has to do with your investment, which has now come to naught. You invested heavily in your child emotionally. Even if you faced difficult days with your child, you developed dreams for his future. As your child grew older, you noted special talents and interests. Your child may have spent time talking with you about what she wanted to be or do upon growing up.

You probably invested financially in those dreams. You

purchased insurance policies to ensure that your child would have enough money when you die. You may have paid for braces, for music lessons. You may have encouraged your child to develop skills in sports or other physical activities. You may have bought calculators or computers to help your child achieve. You may have borrowed money or set aside funds to help your child through college.

Parents would gladly pay it all again, and a thousand times over, if they could have their child back. But that isn't possible. It may help, however, to understand that your financial investment was symbolic of your emotional investment. It may help you understand why a child's death seems so deeply wrong.

Having a child killed is not only to lose someone you feel driven to nurture and protect, but also to lose hopes and dreams for the future.

No words can ever describe the pain of losing a child. On that night in April, 1984, a large part of my inner self died along with my only daughter. All of her hopes and dreams are gone. She will never graduate from high school, go to college, or experience the special love of a husband and children. All those things she spoke of so often are gone, and with them so much of my future. The void will be with me for the rest of my life.

> *Ginger Babb, writing about her 17-year-old daughter, Julie, who was killed*

Mother and Father as Mates

The killing of a child can have a tremendous impact on the marriage of the parents. Some couples find that the tragedy draws them closer together. This can happen when they communicate openly and support each other as first one, and then the other, has bad days. It is common, however, for the marital relationship to break down in the aftermath of a tragedy so great as the loss of a child.

It is very difficult to support and nurture your mate when your own grief is overwhelming. When experiencing trauma, most people regress to a childlike state. They feel vulnerable and need to be taken care of. If both mates are in the same condition, and neither has the strength to care for the other, feelings of alienation will emerge.

This morning, upon my husband's pillow,
A tear.
Last night I heard no weeping,
I felt no rhythmic shaking.
Yet there it is,
Glistening, silent testimony to pain.

Quickly I reached to blot it
As if one swift brush
Could set the world right again.
But something stops my hand,
Stops me to wonder:
Am I the cause of weeping?

In my life is much sorrow,
Dreadful longing and much emptiness
That even my husband cannot fill.
Sorrow brings sleepless nights in fear
Of other phone calls and ambulances;
More longing and emptiness.
My husband shares this loss
But men don't cry.
They nod gravely and tend to details,

Make arrangements and give support.
Yet, there it is upon his pillow:
A tear.

Have I given way to grief
And forgotten one who shares?
Have I made no room for his tears
In the flood of mine?
Am I the reason he weeps
Only in the silence of the night?

I close my hand
To leave the tear drying there.
No more will I blot out his pain
To tend to mine,
For we must share
In order to live—together.

Marcia Alig

Because your drive to nurture and protect has been violently interrupted, you will probably have a strong need to assess blame. As previously discussed, many parents blame themselves and feel guilty. It is also tempting to blame your mate.

If a child has a terminal illness, it is usually no one's fault. Parents can become very angry that science has not found a cure or the treatment was not successful. But when parents are able to care for their child as he is dying, they can know that they did everything they could.

When a child is killed, someone was at fault. If the cause of the death is not explicitly clear, parents may engage in a relentless search for answers. They can usually find a way to blame the other parent, at least in part.

Blaming will intensify the impact of the trauma. It can be a major factor in the breakup of marriage following the death of a child. It may also lead to the premature death of some parents within three to five years after the death of their child.

Another component of stress between mates is the fact that rarely do two people move through grieving in the same way. As a father, you may choose to grieve privately. You may be angry, deeply resenting the loss of control you feel when you think about your child's death.

As a mother, you may be more open with your grief. You want to talk about it, to cry with someone who understands. You may be more sorrowful and wonder how your mate has the energy to be so angry. On another day, these roles may be reversed.

One of you may cry at the mention or even the thought of the child who has been killed. The other may function well enough to return to work. One may read books to better understand what is happening, while the other may refuse to face the tragedy. One may want to go to a support group of fellow sufferers while the other feels repulsed at the mention of it. It is very difficult to understand and accept each other's grieving when they are so different.

> *I felt different emotions than my husband did. I felt compassion for the other driver, feeling his conscience would punish him. My husband wanted him to pay dearly. Then there was, for a time, so much guilt—if Mike had a bigger, faster car, a daytime job-so many "ifs." My husband seemed to have a larger problem with this than I did. I only wished I had said "I love you" more often.*

> *Rita Chiavacci*

Death of a Daughter or Son

A very practical side of these differences has to do with deciding what to do with the child's "things." One parent may be eager to dismantle the child's room and discard clothing and mementos. The other may believe that to do so would deny the existence of the child. Trying to find a happy medium for these polarities may be difficult.

Many couples are distressed to learn that jealousy and envy rear their ugly heads during grieving.

If you are depressed and apathetic and are at home, you may envy your mate who is at work because you fantasize that he or she can be happy there with the many distractions that a job entails. If you are the one working, you may envy the mate at home who can face the grief and not have to "hold up to get the job done."

A father may envy the mother because she carried the child in her body for nine months and birthed it, a closeness with which he is unable to identify.

Mates may have unrealistic expectations of each other regarding workload and maintenance of the home. Sloppy housekeeping or failure to mow the lawn may infuriate a mate who is depending on the other to stay on top of things. Many couples say it takes months before they have enough energy to do more than what simply has to be done.

Sexuality can become a divisive issue during bereavement. Your mate may face an increased need for sex as nurture, escape, or release, while you are repulsed at the thought of it. Avoidance of sex can stem from fear of having and losing other children. It can be rooted in guilt over experiencing pleasure when something so awful has happened. Or it can manifest as a classic symptom of depression.

Chapter 3

If your barriers to feelings are let down in order to experience the closeness of sexual intimacy, then the floodgate is also opened to pain and grief. Since sexual intimacy and orgasm can put you in touch with feelings at a deep level, you may avoid it for fear of tapping into uncontrollably painful emotional release. This can be complicated by the fact that your mate may have mannerisms or physical attributes similar to that of the dead child. To be reminded so potently of the child's death when approaching sexual intimacy can be devastating.

Any of these problems can cause you or your mate to back away from sexual contact. Then the avoidance, if not talked about, can be perceived as additional rejection. For example, your mate may perceive you as unresponsive and totally wrapped up in your grief when you say you are not interested in sex. Your mate may then perceive you as insensitive. In fact, both of you are hurting and are trying to minimize your own unique pain.

Unfortunately, your mate is the easiest target for venting all types of frustrations. You spend many hours together. Your defenses are down more at home than anywhere else. It is important for you to understand that these problems nearly always arise. You will be fortunate if they do not.

When these problems surface, try to understand that they are normal consequences of having your child killed suddenly and violently. You don't feel normal. But you are normal in the sense that pain and struggle following major surgery are normal. A very significant part of your life has been cut out. The process of getting better requires time, patience, and hard work.

An oft-quoted myth is that 80% to 90% of marriages fail when a child dies. Studies reaching this conclusion failed to take normal divorce rates into account and were based on couples already in counseling when their child died. We now know that

Death of a Daughter or Son when divorce does follow the death of a child, it is usually the result of problems that existed before the death. Perhaps the marital problems no longer seemed reconcilable after the death of the child. Some of the positive aspects of living through trauma _ reordered priorities, a sense of endurance, and newfound assertiveness _ may contribute to the decision to go ahead and divorce. In fact, most marriages do survive the death of a child.

How Long Will It Take?

You are no longer the same person you were before your child was killed. To expect that you will ever be exactly the same is to place an unrealistic burden on yourself.

It is also impossible to place a timetable on your grieving. Remember that many factors play into grief, and you will develop your own timetable.

Some parents begin to feel better as they are able to make sense of what happened by learning all the facts. Some begin to feel better after the court case is completed.

Many people say that the second year is harder than the first. Most people feel noticeably better by the third or fourth year, although some say the third year is harder than the second. Research shows that most survivors feel significantly better by the fourth year. There will always be good days and bad days. But the pain will decrease as time goes on. You will one day be surprised to learn that you can feel sad without becoming engulfed in grief. You will find it possible to be happy, if only for a short period of time. Having friends and family who love you and accept you as you are is a blessing. They may be more important than anyone else in helping you heal.

You may want to keep a journal or diary. Journaling is a

good way to see your progress. You may be surprised to learn that what you wrote today shows marked improvement over what you wrote three months ago. It is hard to say when healing starts, but when looking back, it is easier to see.

Suggestions

- Remember that your family is not a "bad family" or your marriage a "bad marriage" because difficult problems arise. It would be unusual if your marriage and family did not suffer. Recovery from the death of a child is one of the most difficult tasks any family can undertake.

- Try to understand that it is rare for any two people to grieve the same way. Pay attention to your own grieving needs and do what feels right for you. Likewise, try to respect the needs of others that live in your household.

- Try to keep talking with your mate and with surviving children about how you feel. Attempting to hide your feelings from your family is like covering a cancer with a bandied. The pain always comes through. You will all be healthier if the pain is out in the open. It is good for you to cry together.

- If your family is unable or unwilling to support you in your grieving, look for a support group of people who understand. Consider the organizations that have been formed to help grieving parents, such as Mothers Against Drunk Driving, Parents of Murdered Children, and Compassionate Friends. Look for a counselor, chaplain, minister, or rabbi with skills in helping people who are experiencing grief following trauma.

- Collect as much information as possible about how your child was killed. This information can be obtained from police reports, autopsy reports, and by talking to witnesses. It is important to collect this data for two reasons: Your mind will rest better if you can "make sense" of the experience; and, through collecting data, blame and responsibility can be placed appropriately.

- When disagreements and misunderstandings occur in your family, try not to vent anger by yelling, screaming, or verbally attacking one another. Own your anger, but try not to target someone else in your family. Say, "I love you" every time you feel even a hint of love. These words will be cherished.

- If sexual needs differ between you and your mate, talk about it and try to reach a reasonable compromise. Hugs and tenderly holding each other can be lifesavers, even when more explicit sexuality may not be possible.

- Consider keeping a journal or a diary. It can be helpful not only in giving you a way to release your feelings, but also in helping you measure your recovery.

- Remember that allowing yourself to feel better does not mean that you are forgetting or being disloyal to your child. It means continuing to grieve but becoming less overwhelmed by it. It means that you believe that life, as it goes on, matters. For your own sake and for others who need and love you, you have a responsibility to try to feel better.

- Have patience. Realize that the traditional "one year of grief" is not enough. Only a combination of time and hard work will lead to resolution of the pain and you will never be to-

tally free of it. How hard you work at it and how long it takes
are up to you.

NOTES

IV

DEATH of a BROTHER or SISTER

Special bond.
Precious relationship.
Profound loss.
Sister. Brother.
Painful void.
Please understand.

Jean Lewis

The death of a brother or sister is a crisis for children as well as adult siblings. Yet they are often neglected grievers. Young siblings are vulnerable to emotional problems following trauma. Interestingly, though, many children seem to cope with trauma better than adults do.

Much of what we understand about adult grieving is also true for children:

- A sudden violent death requires different coping skills than an anticipated non-violent death.

- If a child has emotional difficulties before the death of a sibling, and/or if the family suffers marital discord, the child may be more vulnerable to long-term effects of the trauma.

- If a child's brother or sister is killed at a time when their relationship was troubled, as in sibling rivalry, the death may be more difficult.

- If a child has emotional support from the parent(s) or a major caretaker after the death, and is encouraged to express his or her feelings, the child usually will adjust satisfactorily.

If you are a parent whose child has been killed, you may be needed by too many people. You may find yourself comforting your mate, relatives, or friends because they can't come to grips with what has happened to your family. At some point, their needs can overwhelm you, and you must withdraw to survive.

As you observe your surviving children experiencing the trauma, you may be tempted to put them on a plane or bus and send them off to be with someone else who loves them. You wish you could help them escape the pain, and you feel guilty because you cannot comfort them. Simply "hanging on" yourself may be your top priority or the only task you can handle.

It is best for families to stay together and grieve together after a sudden death. A young child should not witness the total collapse of a parent, but tears that overflow from sadness for what has happened should be shared. It is impossible to go through life without hurting. It would be wonderful if we could promise our children life without pain. We can't. Grieving together will teach your child that ugly and unfair things happen, and that all of you can survive them.

Young children don't just look to their parents as models. They usually believe, at least until they reach adolescence, that parents are all-powerful and all knowing. They will trust you more than ever if you are honest about your feelings and if you do not tell them half-truths about the death of your child. A child who watches a lot of television or sees a lot of movies may have warped ideas about death. Therefore, honest communication can result in valuable lessons for your child.

Like adults, children differ in the way they react to death. Age, ethnic customs, religious beliefs, and the relationship they had with the sibling before death will factor in how they react. How the parent relates to the child in the aftermath of the killing, however, is the greatest determining factor in how the child responds.

Children are not miniature adults. Children have their own distinct way of understanding things. Much of that is determined by how old they are.

Young children differ from adults in that they can endure strong feelings for only a short period of time. As an adult, you may feel that your grief goes on and on. A few years from now you will look back and see that you are better than you were before, but now it may seem that the pain is constant.

A child, on the other hand, grieves deeply for awhile and then seems to be content and carefree. Behavior varies widely from hour to hour. One minute the child may be acting out in a violent burst of anger. The next minute, he may want to play games.

Children grieve on an intermittent basis for years after the death of a brother or sister. As they move through their developmental stages, they will understand death in a new way and grief will return according to their new level of understanding and emotional maturity. Developmental levels vary greatly in children, as do their environments. Therefore, a child's specific age is not always a clear indicator of how she will grieve. The age ranges below should be interpreted very liberally.

Infants And Toddlers

Before the age of three months or so, a baby may be as content with other caretakers as he is with his mother, unless the mother is nursing. He has little, if any, memory of family members when they are out of sight. If a constant caretaker continues to nurture and care for him, he will have minimal reaction to a loss in the family.

As the infant grows, he usually develops anxiety when he is around strangers, a sign that he has bonded to his mother or another major caretaker. From that age on, a child who loses a parent will grieve. He clearly knows the parent and depends on the parent to feed, clothe, bathe, communicate, and play with him. His grief after the loss of a parent may look like a diffused sense of distress. He may exhibit whimpering, loss of appetite, loss of speech if he has learned to talk, and finally, quiet resignation. A toddler is not likely, however, to deeply grieve the loss of a brother or sister unless the sibling has assumed a major caretaking role.

A toddler will absorb the feelings expressed in the home. That is why calm nurturing is important. Explanations about death won't have meaning for him. What the people who love him do is more important than what they say. Holding, cuddling, and stroking him are ways of assuring he will be cared for. They are more important than words.

Ages Four Through Six

A child in this age range is still unable to understand what death is or that it is permanent. It is likely, though, that he or she has discovered dead birds in the yard or has seen something dead that was simply picked up and discarded. A young child may

Death of a Brother or Sister
respond to the death of a sibling, therefore, in a rather matter of fact manner. He may speak of the death of his sibling almost as he would the death of a pet. He may be aware that something bad has happened, but not that it is devastating. This can be terribly upsetting to parents who do not understand that his response is normal for his level of development.

The death of a brother or sister is best explained to a young child in physical terms because his thinking is very concrete. "Your brother was in his car when another car crashed into it. It hit so hard that his body got crushed inside the car. It was broken so badly that his heart stopped working and no one could get it to start up again. So, your brother is not breathing anymore. He can't talk or move anymore. He doesn't have feelings. He can't feel hot or cold or wet or dry. He can't feel happy or sad. His body doesn't feel anything anymore, so we will bury his body in the ground (or whatever your family's choice for final resting place of the body)."

A child this age will have difficulty understanding the concept of soul or spirit. If you believe in a spiritual afterlife, it is still important to explain to your child that his brother or sister's body will be buried or cremated. You might explain that the part that now lives in is the part that was able to love and have feelings.

If your child is told that his brother or sister has "gone to and is now happy with God," but he sees that the family is extremely sad, he may be confused. If he later learns that his sibling is at a funeral home or a cemetery, he may feel betrayed.

Your child aged four through six has a sense of right and wrong, not so much because of an inner sense of morality, but because he has been praised for doing "good" things and punished for doing "bad" things. He still clings to many mystical beliefs based on fairy tales he hears and television shows he watches. Therefore, it is quite easy for him to believe that his brother or sister was killed because he did something bad. If he has wished his sibling would go away _ as all brothers and sisters sometimes do _ he may be convinced his wish was responsible for the death. Most children have death wishes. Your family has been invaded by death. Your child may assume, therefore, that it's his fault.

It is extremely important for your child to know that the death of his brother or sister was not his fault. Explaining death in concrete, physical terms will be helpful to him.

Because your young child is still limited in his vocabulary, especially when it comes to describing feelings, he is likely to try to master his loss through play. You can be supportive to your child if you pay attention to his play, whether it be re-enacting the death, playing funeral, or playing "house." Questions such as, "Why is the little brother crying?" can help your child begin to verbalize what he feels.

At this age, it would not be unusual for your child to develop eating or sleeping problems. As a matter of fact, you can almost expect sleeping problems if your child has heard that his brother or sister "died in their sleep" or that dying is "just like going to sleep."

Bowel or bladder control problems can also return and are fairly common symptoms of emotional stress. Consult your doctor if the problems are intense or last so long that you feel they are interfering with your child's health.

Ages Seven through Eleven

Somewhere in this age range, your child will come to the understanding that death is final and that everyone dies eventually. This awareness can be traumatic for the child because he is still so dependent on his family that he can't imagine surviving without them. He may realize that he, too, will die. This new awareness is frightening for any child. But when his brother or sister, who may be near his own age, has been killed, he must face death intimately. He also now realizes that it is not just old people who die.

My big brother Joshua Erik Jones_ 9 years old_ got hit by a car July 8th, 1985. I feel very VERY SAD. I am very VERY MAD at the man who killed my brother! He was really very very drunk. He does not have to stay in jail very long. And I am mad about that too. That man was very very bad! I hope Josh is learning a lot up with God. I don't like to sleep in my bed with out Josh in the bedroom. I miss Josh very very much. I loved Josh very very much. The end.

Jessica Jones, age 7

For children this age, death is seen as an attacker who intrudes and takes life. Your child may be very fearful that he, too, will be killed. It is a realistic fear, based on what has happened. It would not be unusual for your child to develop fears or phobias about anything related to death. He may complain of physical ailments, withdraw, and become excessively careful and cautious. Children in this age range are more likely to exhibit behavior problems following the death of a sibling, especially if they are the only remaining living child in the family.

If your child is in this age range, he has had more years to experience sibling rivalry, more memories of fights with his brother or sister, and more death wishes.

Chapter 4

Even more than when he was younger, he may feel that he was responsible for the death of his brother or sister. He is not intellectually mature enough to persuade himself of his innocence, so he will need help in correctly assessing blame. As you will recall from previous chapters, parents also struggle with tremendous guilt when a child in the family has been killed.

The child in this age range now has an expansive vocabulary and can think abstractly enough to openly express his pain, fears, anger, and guilt. He is not only sensitive to his own feelings, but he can also enter into the feelings of others. He is able to empathize. He not only needs comfort and support, but he can be a source of comfort and support to others. Doing so will make him feel better. He must never be led to believe, though, that he is responsible for making the family feel better. He is not a parent. He is still a child.

It is important that your child participate fully in the family's grieving. He should be told the truth. If he has never attended a funeral, he should be told exactly what to expect. He should share in decisions about the funeral and in grieving rituals during the months and years following. He should be encouraged to be open in his grieving. And you should not hide your grieving from him.

A word of caution regarding this age range. Witnessing your grief, your child may attempt to replace his deceased brother or sister as a means of helping you cope. You must tell him clearly that no one can replace the child who has been killed, just as no one could ever replace him in your heart.

Avoid putting the child who was killed on a pedestal. It is important for you to remember the child who was killed as realistically as possible. Because of guilt concerning the bad times, it is easy to push those times out of consciousness and recall your child as nearly perfect. This can be devastating for siblings. To them, it appears that you love them less and that they can never measure up to what they witness you expressing about your dead child. This can cause them to withdraw now or later when they reach adolescence.

A child in this age range may have difficulty in school. Grieving children are confused and have difficulty concentrating, much like their parents. If school problems continue, they may be a sign of deeper underlying stress. Professional attention should be sought.

Adolescent Siblings

The developmental goal of adolescence is to "leave home" by separating emotionally at first and then physically. In the process of preparing to separate, your child becomes less family oriented and more oriented toward her peers. She finds out who she is and what she believes by venturing out into unknown territory.

She is insecure, and may be somewhat self-centered in order to compensate. She is suffering many losses as she moves through adolescence: the loss of security of having mother and father make decisions for her, the loss of innocence, and the loss of protection by her family.

Because your adolescent is shaky and insecure, the sudden death of a brother or sister is something she definitely does not want to face. She knows she must, but she may frantically try to escape the inevitable. She faces several dilemmas. She is mature enough to understand life like an adult. But she is more vulnerable than many adults because she is experiencing so many other losses and changes.

A teenager has the capacity for empathy, but because she

is self-centered _ as she has to be in order to become "her own person" _ she may believe that no one has ever felt the deep and powerful feelings that she is now experiencing. Indeed, most adolescents have not experienced anything as devastating as the killing of a brother or sister. While a teen needs to lean on her parents for support, she may be reluctant to let these deep emotions show because she is afraid she will seem child-like again.

Our three boys were hit by a drunk driver. -Dennis and Tim were killed instantly. Jeff survived. It's been six months, and our 16-year-old daughter, Pam, still cannot talk about the boys. My husband and Jeff rarely do.

Ilene Hammon

The adolescent may be struggling with the same issues as the younger child, including guilt over sibling rivalry if she recently had open conflict with the brother or sister who was killed. She may think she should take care of her parents who are devastated, or even try to take the place of the dead sibling. As a bereaved parent, you may be inclined to turn to your surviving adolescent child for emotional support. Such an expectation, if constant, can be overwhelming. It can also impede your adolescent from "growing up," pulling away from family and becoming more intimate with peers.

An additional source of stress for the surviving adolescent sibling is over protection from parents. It is almost impossible for a parent whose child has been killed not to have great anxiety when another adolescent is out with friends. This over protection feels stifling and smothering to the adolescent.

All of these pressures coming together for the surviving adolescent can cause her to become self-destructive and engage in alcohol or other drug abuse, running away from home, or taking risks such as playing "chicken" in an automobile. Flirting with death, so to speak, can be a way of trying to gain control. It can also be an escape. Moving fast, keeping the music loud, and forfeiting reality by using drugs are choices she can make to escape the pain.

As parents of an adolescent who has lost a brother or sister, try to be honest and provide emotional support, but do not be surprised if she needs to escape. Doing so, to some degree, is part of normal adolescent development. It becomes even more understandable when the home is filled with so much pain and she is frightened by her own feelings.

Your adolescent may talk more to her friends about her brother or sister's death than she does to you. She may respond better to another adult who is willing to listen because she does not have to worry about her pain hurting that person as much as it hurts you. You should not be discouraged if she reaches out to someone other than you. That is normal for his stage of development.

Adult Siblings

Most people misunderstand how deeply adult siblings grieve. If your sibling was older, you have shared life with him or her as long as you have had your parents. Even if your sibling was younger, you may not remember life without him or her.

A sibling relationship carries with it a bond that preference cannot sever. When your sibling was killed you not only lost a unique loved one, but you lost that person's role within the family as well. If your sibling was the person who organized the family parties, either someone else must now take on that role or your family will be acutely aware of the absence. If your brother was the peacemaker during family quarrels, someone else must

81

absorb that responsibility. It is normal that you and other siblings will try to "fill in" some of these roles. Some changes may take place quite naturally and easily while others may feel awkward and cause a great deal of conflict within the family.

Part of your role within the family may be related to birth order. If your oldest sibling was killed, you may have lost a caregiver or someone to whom you've always looked up. If the "baby" of the family was killed, you may have lost the one you protected the most. If the age difference was great enough between you and the brother or sister who was killed, you may feel almost as though you have lost a parent or a child.

When a brother or sister dies, you also experience a gap in birth order. If the oldest sibling was killed, the second oldest is now the oldest. If there were just two of you, you are now an only child.

If the sibling killed was your twin or part of a multiple birth, you may be feeling that part of you has died, too. You will need to work hard at rational thinking to prevent you from concluding that the wrong one died.

Many bereaved siblings find it difficult to answer social questions. When someone casually asks, "How many brothers and sisters do you have?" or, "How many are in your family?" you may feel unable to respond. There is no "right" way to answer these questions and you may answer differently from time to time depending on how you feel and the setting in which you find yourself.

Assuming you had three brothers and one was killed, you may want to say, "I have three brothers; two are living, one was killed." You may want to say, "I have three brothers," and leave it at that. On the other hand, you may want to say, "I have two brothers." You have the right to answer these questions in any way you feel comfortable.

For some bereaved siblings, the fact that their sibling's death has altered their relationship with their parents is deeply painful. Chances are, under the stress of coping with the death of their child, your parents will react to you in some ways as though you were still a small child. They are struggling with the sense-lessness and the unnatural order of being predeceased by one of their children.

You may find your parents are trying to comfort you at the expense of themselves, or are trying to protect you from the reality of death. They may be terrified that another family member may be killed and may go to great lengths to monitor your activities. If this behavior is creating a barrier within the family, you may need to talk with your parents and offer them some concrete ways that they can be supportive of you. In turn, invite them to tell you what you could do to comfort them. In times of crisis, it is very easy to fall into old parent/child habits, but it does not have to be that way. They will need to give a little, but so will you.

Similarly, you may find yourself falling into old patterns of behavior in an effort to protect your parents. You may feel they hurt enough without having to watch you grieve. You may go to incredible lengths to hide your pain from them. It may seem right for you to make decisions for your parents or take on paren-tal responsibilities in an effort to care for them. You may end up "parenting your parents." Usually, though, adult children and parents care for one another because it gives them something to do with their grief. Ask if your parents feel you are over-protecting or smothering them. Respect their response and accommodate as best you can.

In some ways, you may feel as though, in addition to the

loss of your sibling, you have lost your parents. Your parents may always have been strong and there for you in times of crisis. Even if you aren't very close to your parents, it can be incredibly painful to become aware of their vulnerability and weakness. This may be the first time you've turned to your parents for support and they can't solve the problem and make it better for you. You may need to grieve the loss of your parents, the parents that were always strong, always in control, never vulnerable.

Ultimately, you will likely forge a new relationship with your parents. Talk with them about what you observe and ask them to share with you how they see you differently. Tell them you want to use these new understandings to build a new, more mature, relationship with them.

Like watching a rock tossed into the lake, you may experience other losses connected with your sibling's death. If your brother or sister married, your family may lose contact with the husband or wife, and with the children. If you want to stay close with them, you may have to be direct about your desires and take the responsibility for staying in touch. Eventually most widows and widowers remarry, which can be extremely painful to the family of the dead husband or wife. Remember, if you can, that no one will replace your brother or sister and remarrying isn't an act of disloyalty. A new spouse will probably be very uncertain about his or her relationship with your family, and will welcome some clarification from you.

If your sibling had children, they will likely be precious reminders of your brother and sister. Discovering traits and physical features in nieces and nephews that are similar to those of your brother or sister is both joyous and painful. Similarly, the special moments in their lives _ graduation, marriage, the birth of a child _ will be bittersweet as they will always highlight your sibling's absence from these events. Children, especially those who were small when their parent was killed, will want to learn about that parent from you and others. Maintaining a relationship with nieces and nephews is one way some bereaved siblings have found to honor the memory of their brother or sister.

If you are married, your own spouse may feel like one of the forgotten victims. Your spouse may have had a very special relationship with your sister or brother, yet he or she does not have the same official ties with your family. Don't forget to include your spouse and the spouses of other brothers and sisters in family events following the death of your sibling. They have also lost the person you were before your brother or sister was killed. While their grief may be different, it needs to be recognized and accepted just as is yours.

Suggestions

- Be careful about explaining death in half-truths to younger children who need honest, concrete explanations of what has happened. If the child hears, "Your sister has gone away for a very long time," he may feel that his sister has deserted him. He may then go on to interpret the desertion as punishment and have strong feelings of guilt. "Your brother has gone to ," is in itself impossible for a young child to understand, especially when he learns that the body is buried in the cemetery. "Dying is like going to sleep," can be a frightening thought for a child and may result in his fear of going to sleep. "Your sister went to the hospital and died," can cause a young child to conclude that hospitals make people die. "Your brother died because he got sick," may cause a child to become extremely fearful of any kind of illness.

- Spend time in play with the younger child who may not have adequate communication skills to talk about his feelings.

- Help your child express his feelings by being willing to express yours. Ask your child questions. If he is reluctant, phrase questions as if they were someone else's, "What would you say to Jimmy if he asked you what happened to your brother?"

- Remember that most children grieve intermittently rather than chronically. Therefore, do not be upset because your child has periods when the death of his brother or sister seems unimportant.

- Children may find it easier than parents to discard personal possessions of the deceased. They may also find it easier to "put their grief aside" and find normalcy in school or play. Remember that your deceased child's friends may be pleased to be given something that belonged to your child.

- Protect young children from witnessing an emotional collapse, but otherwise share as much of the grieving as possible.

- During the early days of grieving, it is helpful for grieving children to have a personal "ally" to provide stability and understanding. This person calms the anxious child and relieves the parents of total responsibility.

- Siblings aged six, seven, or older should be given all the facts about their brother or sister's death as they become known. Not being told the truth only enhances a growing sense of being unimportant in the family.

- If you see another child who reminds you of your child who has been killed, point this out to the siblings and explain the grief spasm it has caused. Mysterious behavior on the part of the parent only enhances the sibling's fear of being left out or of not being loved as much as the deceased child.

- Share your grief with your surviving children, but do not depend on them to take care of you in your grieving. Understand that adolescent children may not want to grieve with you.

- Talk with surviving brothers and sisters both about pleasant memories of the child who was killed as well as unpleasant memories. This will help them to understand that the child who died was not perfect. Placing the dead child on a pedestal can cause great insecurity for surviving siblings.

- Do not ask surviving siblings to "be strong" for you or for anyone else. That is too great a burden to carry.

- Try not to feel threatened if adolescent siblings seek out other adults or peers for support. That is normal for their developmental level.

- As an adult sibling, spend some time focusing on the role of your brother and sister in the family and how you can enable a meaningful transition to the family now. Be gentle with yourself and with your parents.

NOTES

V

DEATH of a MATE or LOVER

The tragic, sudden or violent death of a husband, wife, or lover is among the most stressful of losses. No matter what your age, you are not ready to be suddenly abandoned by the person you depended on the most.

Many books address the death of a spouse. This chapter will focus primarily on aspects of grieving that relate to sudden death.

Roles and Responsibilities

Your mate probably fulfilled many roles in your household and in your life. Your mate was co-manager of your home and co-parent of your children. Together you decided how to spend money, made career decisions, disciplined children, and entertained friends. Your mate may have been your best friend.

If you and your mate shared most of these roles, you may be left feeling overwhelmed by the fact that you now will have to assume sole responsibility.

Some couples choose to separate responsibilities rather than share them. For example, one partner may pay all the bills, maintain the car and yard, decide on major purchases, and do the financial record keeping for the family. The other may be responsible for in-home maintenance, primary care of the children, and entertainment. The sudden loss of a partner can cause feelings of helplessness and vulnerability that make coping extremely difficult. The surviving partner must suddenly assume new roles that may seem awkward and frustrating. To be forced to learn a number of new roles in the midst of grieving is a monumental task.

You may never have operated a clothes washer or dryer. You may never have planned a weekly menu and shopping list. You may not know how to cook. You may be totally ignorant about automobile maintenance. You may not know how to make repairs around the house. You may not know what records to keep for income tax purposes. You may not understand about certain bank accounts, annuities, investments or other financial matters for which you are now responsible.

Frustrations such as these are exaggerated if the surviving partner also assumes sole responsibility for children. The children also are likely to be grieving and struggling with feelings of abandonment.

In addition to all of this, your financial security may be threatened. If the deceased partner provided all or part of the household income, you may face a complete change in lifestyle. See Chapter XI of this book for suggestions in coping with financial matters. These may help you through the first months, but you may eventually need to make major changes in order to be responsible and survive financially.

You can expect changes in the way you are perceived by your friends. If you and your mate shared social relationships with other couples, you may find that you no longer "fit" in the group. If you continue to be included, you may find you feel terribly alone in a group. You may start to feel uncomfortable around other people's mates, fearing your interactions could be misinterpreted. If your social relationships centered on your mate's employment or circle of friends, you may no longer feel you belong.

The absence of physical intimacy is one of the most difficult aspects of the death of a mate. Sexual interest may wane as you grieve, but most people continue to need touching and holding. These yearnings may go unsatisfied until another relationship can be established. Your interest in a new relationship may be the last thing on your mind for some time. But this can change depending on your age and the quality of the previous relationship.

Dependence/Independence

To enhance the healing process, it is important to understand dependence/independence issues as you try to endure the death of your mate. It is usual for two people living together to be emotionally dependent on each other. The degree of dependence you placed on your mate may have a major influence on the state of your grieving.

Some couples are wholly dependent on one another. Each one feels only half of a whole. With the death of the other half, they have difficulty imagining they will ever be able to function alone.

BEFORE

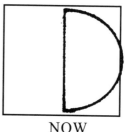

NOW

Some couples shared responsibilities, but experienced themselves as independent individuals who rarely "needed" each other to feel good about themselves. They enjoyed each other, but did not lose a sense of themselves when their spouse died.

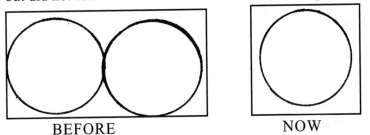

BEFORE   NOW

Other couples felt primarily independent, but realized that each had various aspects of life in which one depended on the other. They experienced both dependence and independence.

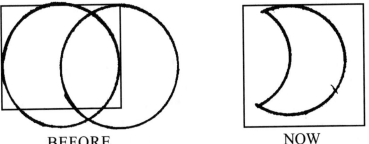

BEFORE   NOW

Mates with some degree of independence generally will cope with the sudden death of a partner better than will those who were excessively dependent. If you were in an emotionally-dependent relationship, you will have the task, eventually, of learning how to be a more independent person. In time, you will shed the image of a "partners other half," and enhance your sense of individuality.

If you successfully moved away from your parents and achieved a sense of independence and autonomy before entering a relationship with your mate or partner, this process may be one of rediscovery. On the other hand, if you were originally dependent on your parents and then became immediately dependent on your mate, recovery may be more difficult.

Rediscovering your own autonomy may require dramatic growth if you decide to work on it at the same time you are grieving the death of your mate. You may find a grief therapist or marital counselor helpful if you feel you are getting stuck. Or you might choose to work in a more slow, quiet way, testing your independence daily until you see that you have reoriented and adjusted.

While such growth and adjustment toward autonomy is tedious and painful, most surviving spouses who have experienced it believe that it is worth the effort. They learn that they can endure independently. Spouses also feel a sense of satisfaction that they can eventually form another relationship out of desire, not need.

How does this kind of growth manifest itself? It can mean moving from indecisiveness to feeling good about independent decision-making. It can mean shifting from helplessness to helpfulness. It can mean replacing intense yearning and sorrow for what you no longer have with celebration of what you had, which you will never lose.

If you were a more independent mate and your partner was killed, your situation likely will be different. You may not feel helpless and indecisive, but you may wonder why you feel so anxious and lonely. Some people need to be needed. Parents nearly always feel some degree of this when their children are small, but the feelings change as children grow more independent. Perhaps you chose to live with a partner who needed you. If so, you may feel unimportant now.

In order to feel better, you may look for other relationships with dependent people. If you send out conscious or un-

Death of a Mate
conscious signals that you like dependent people, you surely will find them.

Perhaps you will want to re-evaluate the pros and cons of an independent-dependent relationship. You may want to consider what it was like for your mate to have been so dependent on you. You may decide that you want future relationships to be different.

Satisfying/Difficult Relationships

All people have some ambivalence in their relationships. In the most affectionate of relationships, couples experience instances of anger, even hostility. However, most relationships are either basically satisfying or basically conflict-ridden.

If your relationship with your mate was generally satisfying, mutually rewarding, and if you have few guilt-producing memories, you will probably cope better in your grief than will others whose relationships were conflict-ridden.

Consider the loss of a satisfying relationship. Looking closely, you may find that although you deeply grieve the death of your mate, you have little about which to feel remorseful or guilty. You have many memories to cherish. You can say that your life together was something to be celebrated.

If your relationship with your mate was conflict-ridden, you may experience some sense of relief from the conflict as the shock of the death wears off, but it may be replaced with a remorse you don't understand. Even though the relationship was negative, the feelings and attachment may have been strong. A difficult relationship is still binding.

You may feel guilty because you weren't able to work things out. You may be obsessed with memories you wish you could forget. Even though you know it's impossible, you long for another chance to make your relationship different. Sometimes the guilt is so painful that you unconsciously repress it and actually forget the hostility you previously felt. What you feel becomes, literally, too much to bear.

This is not unlike what children from unhappy homes experience when they are moved out of their family home and into a foster home. They eventually forget about the abuse and long to return home. They become convinced that problems in the family were their fault and they are sure it would be different if they could be reunited with their family.

Wishing for another chance when you know you will not have it can leave you feeling guilty, depressed, anxious, and yearning for your deceased mate. You may decide consciously or unconsciously that remaining stuck in depressive mourning is the only way you can make it up to your dead mate. Intellectually, you may know this does not make sense, but the feelings can be difficult to overcome nevertheless.

Your task in getting better is to recall honestly both the strengths and weaknesses of your relationship. It is appropriate to be remorseful for failures in your relationship that were your fault. It is likely, however, that you will put your dead mate on a pedestal to counter the ill wishes you had toward him or her in life. You may conclude that problems in the relationship were all your fault. Your task will be to evaluate the relationship rationally. Ask yourself what failures in the relationship were your mate's? What things about your mate did you resent? What did you appreciate? How much of the responsibility should be placed on your mate? How much on you? As you answer these questions, you should be able to set aside some of your irrational guilt and therefore be more able to let go of your mate.

In summary, you are who you are, in part, because of the

relationship you had with your mate. You are now forever changed because of your experiences in coming to grips with the death of your mate.

You will never get "completely over" the relationship or the loss of your partner. It is part of who you are now. Even as you eventually feel ready to begin a new life, you will not forget the past. Your task is to understand the changes that have taken place, accept them, and develop your life in the face of this new reality.

Suggestions for Coping

- Consider the roles and responsibilities that formerly belonged to your mate. Decide which ones you must now assume and which ones are optional. You may decide to find someone else who can take over some of the optional responsibilities. You may decide that some can be let go.

- Do not be hasty in making decisions that involve substantial sums of money. Seek out a trusted friend, relative, or a professional financial advisor to help you make these decisions wisely.

- Make an effort to maintain some social relationships, even if it means discovering new groups or making new friends.

- Acknowledge that you have physical intimacy needs and look for constructive ways to have those needs met. Some people find massage by a legitimate masseuse to be a practical solution. Pets that enjoy being stroked can also be comforting. Even taking care of plants can involve you in intimate contact with living things.

- Evaluate the dependence/independence aspects of your previous marriage or relationship. If you decide you want to make changes in yourself now that you are alone, seek out the kind of help you need to identify and accomplish these changes.

- If your relationship was conflict-ridden, work hard to realistically evaluate it. Be objective about placing the responsibility and do not take more than your share. Identify resentment and appreciation of your mate. Evaluate your own strengths and weaknesses.

- Realize that coming to grips with the killing of your mate will take courage, hard work and patience. Getting better may take more time than you realized. Understand that you are forever changed by what has happened.

- Don't be so frightened of the pain of grieving that you try to escape it by becoming excessively active, entering into other relationships prematurely, or using large doses of medications, alcohol or other drugs. It is best to lean into the pain and fully experience it as you are able.

- Seek out support groups specifically for persons who have suffered the death of a loved one after a tragic death, or for persons who are widowed. You will gain hope for getting better as you see how others have survived, changed, and are coping.

- Understand that you are likely to face other losses, although they are not likely to be as traumatic as the loss of your partner. Try to be aware of your progress in grieving the death of your mate. Identify tools for coping that may help you in the future.

VI

DEATH of a PARENT

Death of a Parent During Adulthood

It is not unusual for an adult's parent to die. Most parents die before their children. Adult children wonder about when and how their parents will die. They feel a great deal of sadness as they see their parents becoming forgetful, frail, and slowing down.

Very few adult children, however, consider the possibility that a parent could be killed suddenly or violently. While they may think about things they want to tell their parents, most adult children put them off, or write them in a Mother's Day or Father's Day card. They feel confidant that at some time in the future, the time will be right to tell their parents how much they love and appreciate them for providing a lifetime of support and encouragement.

Nothing feels right when a parent is killed. Even when the parent is elderly, an adult child can expect the same devastation to be as great as that described in previous chapters of this book. Additionally, the killing of a parent presents some unique aspects of grieving.

The longer your parent lived, the more memories you

have to cherish. Likewise, the more regrets you have about things you did or did not do.

Many people regress to a child-like role when visiting with their parents, even if they are thirty, forty or fifty years of age. Most of us want to share our life's highs and lows with our parent. Even as adults, it is important for our parents to be proud of us.

A significant part of growing up is "cutting the apron strings," becoming independent, and directing your own life. Yet even those who are most successful at becoming independent know that at some level, a part of them will always remain their parent's child.

Thus, when a parent dies, an adult child can feel suddenly void of nurture and guidance. This can be especially true if the parent's death was sudden and violent. Your spouse holds a unique relationship with you that can be a special source of love and caring. Your child, likewise, loves you in a special way. Yet after a parent has been killed, you may realize you were more nurtured than you realized. Having your parent killed may leave you feeling insecure.

Another difficult component of grief after the sudden and violent death of a parent is the loss of dignity. All rational adults hope that their parents will die with dignity. Most hope to be able to say that their parent lived a good, full life, and died peacefully in the presence of loved ones. That seems just after all the parent gave to the child and others in life.

While the "time" is rarely right for anyone's death, it is even more difficult if your parent died a victim of someone's unnecessary violence or negligence. Even if your parent was in some way negligent or responsible for what happened, it does not seem right that a long life could suddenly be snuffed out in an instant. Being killed is not a dignified way to die.

A third difficult component of grief after the homicide or suicide of a parent is the sudden change in roles. Before your parent died, you were the "middle generation." You had a parent or parents. You may have had a child, or at least anticipated having children some day. Suddenly, in an instant, you are the "older" generation. You may, for the first time, see your children as heirs—as you are now forced to become an heir. It is unsettling to think of yourself as the older generation. You do not feel experienced or wise enough to fulfill that role. Thus, even as an adult, you grieve the loss of innocence and dependence. No longer having a parent to lean on, you may feel forced into maturity before you are ready.

How you respond to death depends on many things, including how you have learned to cope with loss, how much emotional support you have in your grieving, and how you are able to maneuver legal matters such as insurance, wills, or civil and criminal procedures. If your parent did not have a spouse and did not leave a will, you may find yourself thrust into a stressful situation with your siblings about what to do with your parent's assets.

Most of all, how you grieve depends on the relationship you had with your parent. The better the relationship, the fewer the regrets and the lesser the guilt. If you were dependent on your parent, however, you may feel more devastated and lost than others. You may experience deep longing for your parent, which seems impossible to resolve. In a sense, you may feel too weak to go on without your parent.

You may experience more difficulty if you had a troubled relationship with your parent. Many children, whether they are young or adult, believe that difficulties with a parent are their fault. Even abused children sometimes spend a lifetime trying to measure up to the expectations of their parents. They believe that one day they will figure out what to do or say that will please the parent and cause the parent to feel proud of them.

If you and your parent did not get along, you may feel guilty for not trying harder to work it out. You may feel a tremendous amount of rage toward the person responsible for your parent's death because your desire to make things better was made hopeless so abruptly.

If you review your past and realize that you spent a lot of time feeling bad about yourself, those hurtful feelings may resurface following the death of your parent. If you feel intensely guilty or empty because you somehow link the death of your parent with your bad feelings, you may want to seek professional counseling. Counseling may help you determine the rationality of your thinking.

Most adults whose parent is killed feel some or all of the above. It is important to face all your feelings and to give yourself time in solitude to both mourn your loss and remember the happy times you enjoyed with your loved one. To do only one and not the other may be to abort part of your grieving.

Society can make it difficult for you to grieve the loss of your parent. More than any other age group, you will be expected to "get on with your life" very soon. It is considered "natural" for adults to lose their parents.

You may be surprised to find that even your best friends will be reluctant to ask how you are or to acknowledge your grief. If you are a child whose parent is killed, you are called an orphan. Many people are concerned about your welfare. If your spouse is killed, you are called a widow or widower. Friends and neighbors are available to offer help. However, there is no name for the adult child whose parent is killed. People seem to minimize your grief, even when your parent has died a sudden, undignified or unnecessary death.

Death of a Parent During Childhood

Much has been discussed about a child's grief in Chapter IV. The reactions of children to the death of a parent and the death of a sibling overlap.

As with siblings, the impact of a parent's death on a child depends much on the child's developmental stage. Children are vulnerable to psychological problems after the death of a parent or a sibling. No one knows for sure why some children cope better than others do. The quality of care taking by the surviving parent or subsequent nurturer may be most important in how a child endures the loss of a parent.

For most children who understand that death is permanent, their initial response to the death of a parent is fear for their own survival. They cannot imagine anyone but their parent putting them to bed, getting them up, feeding, and clothing them. The insecurity of an adult child whose parent was killed has been discussed. For a young child, that same sense of vulnerability is much greater.

Additionally, surviving children may fear their own death. If a child's parent can disappear suddenly and without cause, a child thinks, so can he.

Children tend to see their parents as wise and all knowing, especially prior to adolescence. A child whose parent was killed is forced suddenly to face the reality that the parent was not wise enough or strong enough to prevent being killed. If the parent could be killed, certainly the child can also.

Guilt is a third component commonly present in grieving children. Children know they have angered their parent. They have resented the parent for disciplining them. They may wonder if they were somehow responsible or at fault for the death. They know that their behavior angered the parent from time to time, so they rationalize that perhaps their behavior was responsible for the death as well. If a child believes this, he may feel terribly guilty and wonder if he too might die.

Many people believe that trust is the foundation of a child's emotional development. If a child is fed when hungry, diapered when wet, and nurtured when lonely, he decides, long before he can verbalize, that life is good, the world is safe, and getting his needs met is predictable. The rest of his emotional development depends on that foundation.

The sudden death of a parent can shatter that trust, although it doesn't have to. One of the most complex components of a parent's sudden or violent death is the fact that most or all of the adults in the family are devastated. The remaining spouse, grandparents, aunts and uncles, and other family friends may all be in shock. They may be so absorbed in their own grief that they forget to or can't reach out to the child.

If a child is shuffled from one temporary caretaker to another, he may feel emotionally "out on a limb." He may experience physical neglect and emotional abandonment. He may no longer believe that his needs will be met. Even though he may not fully understand death, it is clear that those who surround him are weak and insecure about what they should do.

Therefore, it is important that a safe, predictable system

of caring for the child be established quickly. This is not a simple task. No one can perform parenting exactly like another. However, if the child knows he can trust someone to feed, clothe, bathe, and love him, he can then participate in grieving with the family. Otherwise, fears for his physical survival, withdrawal, and anger will be primary.

It is equally important for a trusted adult to explain to the child why the parent died. If the cause of death is known, it should be discussed honestly and simply with the child at his level of understanding. The caretaker should tell the truth and answer the child's questions. If it appears that the child feels guilty or is especially fearful and anxious, the child must be made to realize that his parent's death wasn't his fault.

Misunderstandings about these issues can cause a child to be afraid and angry because his life is out of control. However, if he believes that he will be cared for, that the death was not his fault, and that he is not likely to die soon, he will likely endure in a healthy manner.

It must be remembered though, that as a child matures, he may need to grieve a parent's death repeatedly based on new developmental understandings. Life changes that are normally stressful for children may be even more difficult for the child whose parent has been killed. Adolescence, re-marriage of the surviving parent, leaving home, and facing deaths of other loved ones can be tumultuous.

Suggestions For Adult Children Whose Parent Was Killed

- Be prepared for the fact that few people, if any, will understand the trauma you experience when your parent is killed.

- Look for ways to honor your parent with the dignity his or her death lacked. Establish a memorial fund or trust to honor your parent. Write a memorial or poem about your parent's life and share it with others.

- If you had a troubled relationship with your parent, write letters to him or her expressing your feelings. Write a letter to yourself from your parent explaining how you think he or she saw the problem. These letters form a "grief work journal" that can help you adjust and heal. Writing can also help you decide how much guilt is appropriate. If you still find it impossible to be rational about your relationship with your parent, consider professional counseling.

Suggestions For Surviving Spouses or Other Caretakers of Children Whose Parent Has Been Killed

- Maintain a routine for the child that is as stable and consistent as possible.

- Try to ensure that the mode of discipline to which the child is accustomed remains the same.

- If the surviving parent is so preoccupied with his or her own grieving that the child and his needs become an irritant, ask someone to come into the home for several weeks or months to share the parenting load. This is preferable to sending the child away, which can make the child feel even more abandoned and fearful.

- Avoid becoming dependent on the child for your own nurture. While your grieving can be shared and can bring you closer to each other, the child will sense your neediness if you become too dependent. It is too big a load for a child to carry.

- Be alert to persistent fears, anxieties, guilt, or anger. Acting out behaviors such as temper tantrums, clinging, or daydreaming in school or at home may be cries for help. Seek counseling for your child if necessary.

NOTES

VII

DEATH of a FRIEND or COLLEAGUE

In this mobile and disconnected society, friends and co-workers are sometimes more intimate with one another than family. We can be transparent with a good friend, sharing all our secrets and taking off our masks. Perhaps you told your friend things you couldn't tell your parents or your spouse.

Many men and women have affairs outside their marriages. The nature of these relationships dictate they never be openly acknowledged. When a partner in an extramarital relationship dies suddenly, the other is left totally alone and isolated, perhaps unable even to attend the funeral. At best, the relationship is considered a friendship by others.

By law, gay and lesbian partners are considered no more than friends in most states. Imagine the emotional turmoil when one partner dies suddenly after thirty years in relationship.
Ex-spouses often remain good friends, particularly if they continue to co-parent their children. Because others perceive that the death of your ex-spouse makes your life simpler and happier, no one acknowledges your grief. You probably will not have the opportunity to share in planning the funeral because the new

spouse is the "legitimate" mourner. The death of an ex-spouse, however, cannot simply be glossed over. You invested much of yourself, even if the marriage dissolved years ago.

A close, meaningful, and powerful relationship has become suddenly gone. This same relationship may have had the power to change your life or help direct your goals. Because your friend was not a family member, he or she may have had the wonderful quality of caring for you unconditionally while objectively confronting you with things you could not see.

When your friend or colleague died, you may have not been considered a legitimate" mourner by the law, the funeral industry, your employer, or the family. Even though you may have been closer to the deceased than a brother or sister, you may have sat alone at the funeral. No floral shops rang your doorbell. You were not eligible for bereavement time at work other than a few hours to attend the funeral.

To some degree, you may have accepted society's label as a disenfranchised mourner. In fact, you may now be assuming the role of supporting the "real" family. You may prepare food and help take care of other material needs for them.

Among the most ignored mourners are those whose work environment lends itself to frequent exposure to death. If you are involved in police work, hospice care, trauma hospitals, or other settings where death is common, your own colleagues, friends, and relatives may assume you are accustomed or even callused to death. Therefore, when your own friend dies, you are expected to buck up and handle it in the routine manner for which you are trained. Your special relationship with the deceased is not acknowledged.

As you struggle to stifle your mourning at work, you may find your supervisor intolerant of your diminished work production. Because you may be experiencing many or all of the grief symptoms and mourning reactions noted in the first two chapters of this book, you are traumatized. Yet no one seems to notice or care. Indeed, if they notice, you may be criticized. Common reactions to grief that can affect your work include exhaustion, withdrawal, difficulty concentrating, and irritability. Grief can turn into depression. Fear can turn into anxiety or panic attacks. If you experienced or learned of the death at work, simply walking past the area where the death occurred or where you received the tragic information can trigger grief spasms.

If your deceased friend was a work colleague, others may share your grief, even if it is only in the break room. Seek out those who seem to be mourning with you and get together outside the work environment. Share your memories of the one who died and talk openly about your appreciation and regrets. This acknowledges the reality of what happened and provides the social support you need. It may even be possible to organize a short-term support group at work. Meet together during lunch or for an hour before or after work. Talking about your grief makes it more manageable. Realizing that you are not alone in your grief can relieve some of the burden. You may decide to ask your supervisor if your colleague's desk can remain vacant for awhile, a tribute to his or her life. You may even want to place flowers or other mementos on your colleague's desk. Some people have filled the desk with snapshots and other photos of the deceased person.

If your deceased friend did not work where you do, you may find yourself totally isolated at your job. Your colleagues are not likely to respect your mourning and lack of productivity. You must be honest with them. Explain the nature of the severed relationship to your supervisor. Use words "like a brother or sister" if that is true. While you may not be granted bereavement leave, you may want to take a few days of personal leave to go to the cemetery, write in a journal, or seek professional counseling.

A counselor who specializes in traumatic grief can be of significant help if you cannot find someone to recognize the depth of your loss.

Regardless of where you go for support, your task is to get a few other people to recognize and validate your grief. Tell them what you need. Ask that they allow you to talk about your friend. Ask them to look at your photos and listen to your poems. Perhaps someone will be willing to visit the cemetery with you. You can further legitimize your mourning by making a memorial donation in the name of your friend. The receiving organization or charity will acknowledge your gift to the family, which will remind them of your special relationship with your friend.

If you have the physical and emotional energy, consider a public event of some kind. After her good friend was shot to death while at work in San Francisco, Kimberly Rowland organized a march against the use of handguns. The project, which received significant media attention, provided a way for Kimberly to make a significant statement about the value of her friendship.

SUGGESTIONS FOR COPING

- Identify a short phrase that describes your relationship with your friend or colleague such as "like a brother or sister to me" or "closer to me than any of my relatives" to help others understand the significance of your relationship. Use it often.

- Let the family members of the one who died know how special the relationship was to you. This can be achieved through personal visits or a letter that includes stories and photos about your relationship. Except for clandestine affairs, these offerings are likely to be warmly received.

- Visit the cemetery or use other rituals to help you

acknowledged the legitimacy of your relationship.

- While you cannot expect your work environment to provide all the support you need, tell your supervisor about the nature of your relationship and acknowledge your work deficits. If you are unable to work productively, ask for a few days of personal leave.

- If you are unable to find a few people with whom you can honestly and openly share your mourning, seek out a counselor who specializes in traumatic grief.

- Find a way to create something positive from your loss. This may be a donation, publication, memorial, or an activity. Use your own creativity to decide what might best memorialize your relationship.

VIII

SUICIDE

Following a loved one's suicide, you may feel shock, agonizing sadness, guilt, anger, and confusion, perhaps more intensely than you ever would have thought possible. Almost everyone is perplexed, bewildered and overwhelmed when confronted with suicide. While your response to the suicide may be similar to those whose loved one was a homicide victim, it probably differs in several ways.

Like homicide, suicide results in the sudden, irrevocable end of a loved one's life. You may long to say, "I love you," "I'm sorry," or "Good-bye." If your loved one wrote a suicide note, you may anguish over not being able to respond.

An American dies at his or her own hand every seventeen minutes. Teenage suicide is escalating at an alarming rate in the United States. Suicide is the third leading cause of death for fifteen- to twenty-five-year-olds. It is estimated that more American Vietnam War veterans have committed suicide than the 58,000 plus service personnel actually killed in combat. Elderly men are at high risk for suicide. In August 1991, Derek Humphry's book, Final Exit, reached the *New York Times* bestseller list for advice books. To date, it has sold more copies than any other book on suicide. Knowing these facts may be of little comfort to you, however. You are probably focused on potent and bewildering feelings rather than on facts.

Chapter 8

Some people commit suicide violently. Others choose overdoses, inhalations, or other less violent forms. How it happened and why it happened might be of great interest to those who attempt to comfort you, but what probably matters the most to you is that someone you love is no longer alive. In time, you too will focus on the facts, but it is not likely to be your initial concern.

Many people have a need to understand why a person committed suicide. Being able to understand the reason for the act helps survivors to feel less vulnerable. If they can conclude that it was someone else's fault, that someone "missed the signals," or that a legitimate reason for the suicide existed, then it makes some sense.

You likely will be inundated with questions from family members and friends. Try to be patient. If you don't feel like answering questions, simply say, "I appreciate your interest. Perhaps one day I can talk about `how' and `why,' but right now I'm just sad and lonely and that's all I can face right now."

Denial and Confusion

There must be a mistake. He couldn't have committed suicide. He wouldn't do this to me.

> *Anne Seymour, whose close*
> *friend committed suicide*

The most devastating component of the suicide and the aspect responsible for much denial is that it was your loved one's choice to die. It seems impossible that he or she was so miserable or felt so unloved and hopeless that suicide was seen as the only escape. Confusion and bewilderment may envelop you as you struggle to come to grips with your grief. You will never be able to know all the factors that contributed to your loved one's choice.

Some people take comfort in the fact that the suicide was a choice. In the midst of sadness and confusion, they find solace in the fact that the victim was "in charge" and clearly chose to end his life. If the victim was in physical or emotional torment, the suicide may have been a relief. Since no two suicides are alike, and no two responses to it are alike, only you can decide if any element of relief exists for you. If others believe that you should feel relieved, tell them that only you can decide how you feel.

Anger

I'm so mad at him that I could kill him! I'm angrier than I was with the drunk driver who killed my godchild because that guy was a stranger.

Anne Seymour

It is not likely that your loved one committed suicide to hurt you or to get even, although that is sometimes the case. He or she likely committed suicide to escape an anguish and torment so overwhelming it is impossible for most of us to imagine. The person was probably so consumed by his own sense of overwhelming physical, emotional, and spiritual pain that he chose to end life to escape the pain. Or perhaps the person was withdrawn and depressed, and developed tunnel vision. Life's problems may have taken on overwhelming proportions and there seemed no way out. He likely became so self-focused that little thought was given to others.

In some cases, suicide is manipulative. If you sense that your loved one's suicide was committed in an attempt to prove something, your anger may be ferocious. Did she mistakenly think she was unloved? Did she do this to convince you of something? Did she think she was too weak to endure disappointments or other life problems? Didn't she see how painfully unfair this would be to you? Didn't she think about the hurt and havoc you would suffer in trying to pick up the pieces? The questions go around and around in your head.

You may be angry with yourself as well. You may torture yourself by ruminating over missed signals or your perception that you failed to take the signals seriously. You may have thought of yourself as an aware, caring person, but now feel ashamed and degraded that you allowed this to happen. You conclude that you didn't know your loved one as well as you thought you did. How you felt about your loved one and how he felt about you are now called to question. Your self-esteem may tumble.

You may also find yourself angry with others who seem to blame you. Remember that people less close to the victim than you may be looking for answers. Often the first hypothesis reached is that you were not a good parent, spouse, lover, child or friend. How unfair! Moreover, they may be looking to you to make sense of a senseless act. Without a doubt, even the victim could not have explained exactly why he chose to end his life. Nor should such an explanation be expected of you, no matter how well you knew and loved him.

You will greatly complicate your grieving if you attempt to suppress your anger. It is a reasonable and appropriate response to what has happened. While you may not choose to make other people miserable with your anger, you need to stay in touch with it and express it with those close to you who are able to accept your feelings. As stated in previous chapters, leaning into your feelings and working through them will result in relief more quickly than will suppressing your feelings.

As time goes on and as you express your anger, you also will be able to assess the situation more realistically. With the help of an accepting friend or a professional counselor, you can weigh the positive and negative attributes of your loved one, and you can better assess your relationship. Evaluate the rationality of your thoughts and work toward discarding irrational beliefs about your role in the suicide. This takes time and is hard work. Be patient with yourself.

Guilt

If your loved one tried to reach out to you before the suicide and you weren't available, you may feel over-burdened with guilt. You may be convinced that if only you had been there, the suicide could have been prevented.

You may feel guilty for not having taken the suicide instrument from your loved one, whether it was a gun, a rope, pills or an automobile. If the suicide instrument was something you gave or purchased for the victim, you may irrationally conclude that the suicide was your fault.

Those who experience some relief because of the suicide may feel guilty for these feelings. Your religious training or ethical beliefs about suicide may make it more difficult to reconcile your sense of relief.

A SURVIVOR'S EXPERIENCE

After the suicide of a loved one, one woman wrote:

I left the hospital like a zombie, with little recollection of how I drove the thirty miles home.
The car soon became my "raging place." I found I could cry and scream without disturbing anyone else. So I

screamed. The vocal noises sounded eerie, like a wounded wild animal. I did not know where they came from or who they belonged to, only that they needed to come out.

Weekly, I drove to the therapist. I passed smiling people and wondered what there was to smile about. The "if onlys" haunted me. I felt like a rat in a Kubler-Ross laboratory. Trapped in a grief-maze with no way out, I bounded from one stage to another and back again. I made monthly pilgrimages with floral tokens to the remote hill where his ashes were scattered. I'd stand on the hill and scream,"WHY?"

As I sat in the Mental Health waiting room I could observe other patients and identify with their individual pain. Although I had previously done social work, this was a new chapter in empathy. "They" were no longer separate from "me." It was "us" ...the human condition creating the common denominator.

It was four months before I began to let go. Suddenly, I became aware of what the inside of the therapist's office really looked like. I had never noticed the plants or the furniture, and thought that they were new.

I came home and put together a brick/rock pathway, and felt good for the first time in months. I remembered from somewhere that depression was blocked creativity _ my sidewalk looked beautiful to me.

The weekly trips to the therapist lasted nine months. Eventually I saw that screaming 'why' on a hilltop made no more sense than a three-year-old throwing a tantrum. Then one night as I was soaking in the tub, I looked up on the bathroom wall and admired a large sampler my daughter had embroidered. I had it framed years ago and thought it quite an accomplishment for a fourteen-year-old. Often I had read it. It was the old Serenity Prayer:

"God grant me the serenity to accept the things I cannot change.
The courage to change the things I can....
And the wisdom to know the difference."

I mused a moment"I wonder what the wisdom to know the difference really means?" Suddenly, it came. It meant the ability to know and accept my own limitations.

As badly as I had wanted it, I could not make a life choice for him. In respect for his dignity I finally allowed that he alone had made that choice, and that the choice was a human one. If humans are not perfect, then neither are their choices.... and who am I to judge? Rest in Peace. All is forgiven...finally.

B. H. B.

Human beings have an almost innate conviction that they should be able to protect those whom they love. While that is impossible and irrational, it is difficult to overcome. You can not assume responsibility for an act that was someone else's choice.

It is likely that little could have been done to dissuade the victim from taking his own life. If you were not present when your loved one reached out for help, he would have sought out someone else if he truly wanted to stop himself from succeeding. If warning signals were given, they probably were hidden in ambivalence. If a gun had not been available, a rope or other instrument would have been sought.

Chapter 8

In coming to grips with your guilt, your task is to transfer your focus to rational thinking. Understand that suicide is extremely complex and the act of suicide was only one component of a much greater whole. Many internal and external forces merge in making suicide someone's choice.

Try to determine what proportion of the responsibility may actually have been yours. The extent is apt to be small if it exists at all. Like all human beings, you are not perfect and will need to forgive yourself for any fault that you can logically claim. You probably will find that you made the best choices you could based on the information available at the time. The greatest proportion of responsibility lies with the victim who made a choice to end his life.

Stigma

Suicide is little understood by the public. Some people think that only the mentally or emotionally ill commit suicide and that mental and emotional illnesses are inherited. They may conclude, therefore, that as a relative of the victim, you also are unbalanced and a poor risk for friendship. Some people think that suicide is purely environmental, that you or someone else "drove" your loved one to death. You may therefore be shunned because of the incident, your family history, or personal lifestyle.

Suicide is not a disease. It is not an act of immorality. It is not a biological anomaly. It is not a neurological dysfunction.

In order to avoid the stigma, some people choose to live a lie about the suicide. They tell others that it was an accident or death due to natural causes. While this may be comforting at first, it can greatly complicate grieving. As previously noted, much confusion surrounds the suicide experience. Choosing to lie about the suicide enhances the already existing confusion with the stress of knowing one thing to be true internally and telling a dissonant story externally.

Although it is sad that as a family member or friend of a suicide victim you face ostracism, it is usually a preferable alternative to disguising the truth. Simply stated, people who live lies usually get sick. They begin to suffer physical symptoms and find themselves depressed. They do not want to talk about a cover-up and they will not be able to talk about the truth.

Talking realistically about what happened and sharing your feelings honestly with trusted and accepting friends or family members is your best prescription for recovery. A minister, priest, rabbi, or a professional counselor can be consoling, and it may be wise to pursue this kind of help.

Second Victimization

As newspaper reporters, coroners, insurance representatives, law enforcement officers, and lawyers probe for answers about the suicide, you may feel that your integrity and moral character are being questioned. If you were close to the victim or if you were due an inheritance or insurance money at his death, you may find yourself a murder suspect or an accomplice to the suicide. At the very time you need to be treated with dignity and compassion, you may have to face accusations that can enhance your guilty feelings and reap even more havoc on your self-esteem.

Regardless of your treatment, it is in your best interest to cooperate fully with authorities. Remind yourself that their role is to determine the facts surrounding this sudden death. Most of them have had no training in the dynamics of bereavement following suicide and many are afraid of dealing with emotions.

In order to overcome the powerlessness you may feel in facing these people, ask for documentation of their findings. Get the investigating officer's name and phone number and call from time to time until his report is complete. Ask for a written copy of the completed report and, if you see errors, call to correct them immediately.

If an autopsy was performed, obtain a copy of the report. Autopsies often unveil heretofore-unconsidered rationales for the suicide, such as bodies racked with pain, disease, or high concentrations of alcohol or other drugs. Not all states require autopsies on suicide victims, so don't expect one to be performed automatically. In an era when Acquired Immune Deficiency Syndrome (AIDS) is feared to an almost irrational degree, medical personnel are likely to resist autopsies in cases where a tremendous amount of blood was lost, especially if the victim was considered a high risk for AIDS.

The media can become an insatiable pest, especially if the victim was well known in the community and if any mystery surrounds the death. You have the absolute right to refuse to talk to the media if that is your choice. Rather than responding "No comment," which may create an even more suspicious tone to the event, it is usually wise to give a one- or two-sentence statement. For example, you may want to say, "We are experiencing great grief because of the death of our loved one and choose to refrain from public comment at this time." Such a statement can also be written and given to members of the press.

If you are pestered by members of the press or find that your boundaries are not being respected, call and speak to the news director at a television station or to the managing editor of a newspaper. The telephone numbers can be found in your area telephone directory. State your concerns firmly and in as few words as possible. Be specific and provide names when possible
The legal implications of a suicide can be extremely complex. Some insurance companies may be eager to classify acci-

dental deaths or homicides as suicides in order to avoid paying survivor benefits. Heirs may be eager to prove that the victim was unstable at the time if changes in the will did not benefit them. Many suicide victims leave holographic (handwritten) wills as their Final Will and Testament or as a codicil (amendment) to another document. Their financial and legal matters are often in disarray as a result of depression and confusion. Various family members may be eager to handle or interpret documents, each in a manner that will be the most self-serving. All of this can be frustrating to those who loved the victim and are grieving. Under these circumstances, it is usually prudent for all involved in the financial or legal affairs of the victim to retain professional counsel.

Sometimes, a close friend was more intimately involved with the victim than family members. Friends sometimes sense the signals of suicide, are recipients of the suicide note, and discover the body of the victim. All too often such friends are excluded from family grieving rituals and find themselves awkwardly placed in an adversarial position with the family if they are named as heirs in the will of the deceased. If families can be sensitive to the emotional needs of friends who are equally devastated, they too, will find support through the common bond of shared grief.

God and Suicide

Some people may feel compelled to share their theological positions on suicide with you after the death of your loved one. Your own spirituality may be shaken. You may realize you want more information and time before deciding how you feel about such weighty issues. Please read the Spirituality chapter on page 125 for more information on the subject.

In the meantime, the following information may be useful: Six cases of suicide are mentioned in the Old Testament of the Bible. Nowhere does it forbid suicide. According to Jewish law, however, suicide became considered wrong because life was to be valued.

Likewise, the New Testament of the Bible does not directly forbid suicide. In fact, in the early years of the Christian church, it was sometimes considered a form of martyrdom. By the fourth century, however, St. Augustine categorically rejected suicide because it precluded the possibility of repentance. He argued that it also violated the Sixth Commandment: "Thou shalt not kill."

Theologians and philosophers from that time on have debated the subject of suicide in the absence of clear definitive statements in the Bible. Many point out that Jesus and the New Testament writers placed great emphasis on the forgiving Spirit of God. In asking Christians to forgive "seventy times seventy" _ or infinity _ Jesus reminds us of the abundantly forgiving nature of God.

Perhaps you will want to tell people who seem eager to condemn your loved one that you need time to sort out this issue for yourself, and in the meantime, you believe God is still forgiving.

A Word About Surviving Children

Much of what has been written in this book about the response of children to homicide also holds true for children who experience the suicide of someone they love (See Chapter IV). Children old enough to understand what death is need to be told the truth about how it occurred. Being lied to feels like being excluded from the family. When the truth comes out on the playground or in the neighborhood and the child knows he is not supposed to know, he may feel betrayed and angry. Children respond with guilt, anger, and confusion. Their feelings should be discussed and accepted just like those of adults.

Children sometimes believe that they were mysteriously responsible for the death of their loved one, especially if they had wished the loved one dead (as most children do from time to time). It is obvious that the suicide victim was distressed and unhappy. It is extremely important that children be told all they can understand about the unhappiness and suffering the victim endured, so they don't assign the blame to themselves. Guilt needs to be addressed specifically. The victim did not choose to end his life because the child was bad. The victim did not choose to end his life because the child was not with him. The victim did not choose to end his life because the child could have prevented it and did not.

Since children model after the adults in their lives, especially parents, they will need education and instruction about suicide. They will need to hear time and again that suicide is not a good choice for failure or a way to solve problems. Tell them repeatedly that suicide is not a good way out of disappointment or depression, which can overcome.

Repeated Suicides Within A Family here is a higher incidence of suicide in families that have experienced a previous suicide. Suicide potential is greatest for elderly white males, especially if they are sick or lonely. Social isolation coupled with alcohol or other drug use is a risk factor. Those widowed by suicide are at an even greater risk. Whether this is the first suicide in your family or a repeated event, you can help prevent this from happening again. Enable the people in your family to develop positive problem-solving strategies. It is important to build strong bonds of caring and support with each other, your religious institution, and community groups.

Don't allow a depressed person to withdraw and isolate. Identify the warning signs and engage in conversation. Most people contemplating suicide are still undecided and willing to talk about it. Watch for what may look like improvement in their frame of mind. Most persons who commit suicides do so after somewhat of a lift from despair. It is then that they have the energy to complete it. Look for tunnel-vision or rigidity in thinking. This constriction, seeing no way out of unbearable psychological pain, is the hallmark of suicide.

FOR MICHAEL

Dear Michael with the dancing eyes,
We wonder how your eyes got so blue -
How it was that you were such a handsome lad -
Why it was that you could always make us laugh.

We don't know.

We wonder why you found delight as a little boy
In decorating the kitchen floor with soap
Or flour or spaghetti
Or covering the walls with Avon lipsticks
Or filling our hearts with joy.

We don't know.

We wonder where you got the drive to hit
The winning home-run,
The flair to tell the funniest joke,
The talent to be a fine carpenter,
The compassion to love your little daughters so.
We don't know.

We wonder about the pain in your heart,

If your romance with death began
When your brother was killed,
          If death was your solution of
          choice to ease the tormen,t
If this was your final act of taking responsibility.

We don't know.

We don't know why...
We will never know why...
We don't have to know why.

We don't like it...
We don't have to like it...
We will never again be the same.

But we do have a choice about what we do with it.
Let us not ponder on the road not traveled -
Let us not become destroyed, and thereby destroy -
Let us not try to explain the chaos of our world.

Instead, let us remember
that memories survive,
that goodness lives,
and that love is immortal.

Janice Harris Lord, with
gratitude to Beckie Brown
and Iris Bolton

Suggestions

- Focus on your feelings rather than on the "why" and "how" immediately following the suicide. Understand that it is normal for you to grieve deeply and to experience confusion about what has happened.

- Understand that it is normal for you to be angry with the victim, yourself, and others in the aftermath of a suicide.

- As guilt becomes a problem, immerse yourself in the facts. Obtain copies of all reports, talk with witnesses, family members and friends. This will help you regain control, and own only the portion of the blame that is reasonable. Understand that you will never discover all the answers.

- Don't let people tell you how you should feel. Your feelings are your own.

- Understand that you may be ostracized in the aftermath of the suicide and there is little you can do about it except talk openly and honestly about what happened.

- If you are involved legally or financially, retain counsel.

- Remember that the victim made the decision to commit suicide.

NOTES

IX

HOLIDAYS

We were driving home Thanksgiving and I was thinking about Christmas and how hard it would be. I knew we needed to get it out of our systems and cry and then have a good time. So for Christmas I gave my parents a picture of Kurt and a poem that said, "If I were here all I'd say is - I love you." We all had a good cry. This Christmas was a little better.

A friend sends me flowers on Kurt's birthday, It's nice to know that someone remembers and isn't afraid to remember with me.

The YMCA basketball program has a memorial for Kurt. I remember a card from one of Kurt's friends who had moved from the city. The card said, "Kurt, it is hard for us with you gone. We love you." Remembering is important. You still need to celebrate what their lives meant to you, even as you celebrate your own life.

> *Kim Keyes, whose son, Kurt was killed by a drunk driver*

Your family, and approximately two million others, may lethargically stumble through the holidays this year because someone you love has died. If your loved one was killed senselessly, coping with the holidays may be even more difficult.

Chapter 9

Thousands whose loved one was killed more than a year ago desperately hope that this holiday will be better than the last one.

The holidays can be a cruel reminder of your deviance from the American family ideal. A heightened sense of sadness and loneliness is likely as magazines and television programs focus on intact families gathered around the holiday table or the Christmas tree to celebrate the year's most festive holidays together. Spring may be difficult because it brings Easter, signs of new life, Mother's Day, Memorial Day, Father's Day. You may feel that all your friends are abandoning you because they can't cope with you and your loss during the holidays.

As one mother said, "It seems like everyone is afraid to mention my child's name, probably because they think it will upset me. They need to understand that I will never forget, whether they mention him or not. I desperately need a way to make my child's memory a part of the holiday season. It is senseless to think that I could forget, especially at this time of year."

Support groups such as Mothers Against Drunk Driving (MADD) set aside a special time during the holidays to remember their loved ones and hope for a less violent future. MADD conducts Candlelight Vigils in early December. They are simple; some music, a few brief statements. The most significant aspect of this annual ritual is when families come forward to light a candle in remembrance for a loved one. Tears flow, but as one father says, "It's the loveliest way I know to say Merry Christmas and to acknowledge the joy that Janie brought to us for the seven holiday seasons we were all together."

MADD then follows its Vigils of Remembrance with numerous programs to prevent drunk driving during the holidays. Red ribbons on cars remind travelers not to drink and drive. Other programs include safe-rides programs, designated driver programs, and media campaigns.

Families who have walked a similar path on which you tread offer the following suggestions to help prevent feelings of devastation from becoming more potent than feelings of celebration. They are shared in the spirit of hope that things will get better. They are not given as absolutes, but are intended to trigger thoughts and ideas for each family's unique situation.

Openly Discuss Traditions

To plan a holiday exactly like it was before your loved one was killed is an invitation for trauma. Call the family together and make the holiday plans according to the wishes of the survivors who are hurting the most.

Create a Special Tribute For the Day

Some families find it meaningful to light a special candle on a holiday table, put treasured remembrances on paper on a decorated table, or release helium filled balloons at sunset. Allow your own creativity to develop an appropriate memorial for your loved one.

Plan Where to Spend the Holidays

Many people think going away will make the holidays easier. This may be helpful if "going away" means going to another family member's home where you will feel loved and nurtured. However, If going away means trying to avoid the holiday atmosphere, remember that American holidays are celebrated throughout the country and Christmas is celebrated in many parts of the world. It is usually better to face the pain. Many families are surprised to learn that the fear of facing the holiday is worse than the actual holiday.

Balance Solitude With Sociability

Grief is draining and solitude can help renew strength. Friends and family, however, can be a wonderful source of support, especially if they accept you as you are and do not tell you how you should feel. If you are invited to holiday outings, make an effort to go. If there are musicals or events that you enjoyed before your loss, go to them. If you surprise yourself by enjoying them, wonderful! You may feel like crying later, but you have taken a step in the right direction.

Relive Pleasant Memories

To go through a holiday pretending that nothing happened is a heavy and unrealistic burden. Remember holidays past when your loved one was happy and full of life. Pick out three particularly happy memories. Celebrate and be happy for those times. If feelings of sadness pop up at inappropriate times, such as at work when a task must be completed, STOP yourself from thinking sad thoughts and think about the three happy memories you can celebrate. It won't always work, but it is worth the attempt.

Set Aside Some "Letting Go" Time

Set aside time on your calendar to be alone and "let go" of the sad and lonely feelings. These may be times for crying, writing about your thoughts and feelings, or pretending that your loved one is in the room as you say out loud some of the things you wanted to say while he or she was alive. When special times are set aside for grieving, it will be easier to postpone the flow of grief in public places where a release of emotions could be embarrassing.

Counter the Conspiracy of Silence

Family members may consciously or unconsciously conspire to avoid mentioning the person who has been killed. This is usually a loving and misguided attempt to protect your feelings. If this seems to be happening, take the initiative by mentioning your loved one. This will alert the rest of the family that it is important to you to remember him or her and that doing so will not devastate you. Creating a special tribute or setting aside a few minutes to share memories will help everyone to release their feelings and thoughts.

Try Not to "Awful-ize"

Some people in grief assume "life is awful" during the holiday season. To conclude "everything about life is now awful" is to take some tragic personal experience and generalize irrationally. Although you will have difficult times during the holidays, you can also experience joy. Accept the love and caring of others. Reach out and care for someone else. Feeling good does not mean you have forgotten your loved one or that you loved him or her less. Give yourself permission to feel sad. Also give yourself permission to experience joy.

Find a Creative Outlet

Many people in grief have a strong urge to create. If you feel creative, do something. Write a memorial poem or story and share it. Consider the things your loved one cared about and contribute to an appropriate organization or cause in his or her honor. Some families choose to set aside the money they would have spent on the loved one and buy gifts to take to less fortunate children, a hospital, or a nursing home. One mother baked gingerbread houses at Christmas time. Although she said she was unable to bake the first year after her children were killed, she was able to do so the second year and years after. She baked the houses and gave them as gifts to friends

Consider the Needs of the Remaining Family

131

Chapter 9

Concentrate on the children. Listen to them. Celebrate them. They may have deep feelings that will be overlooked if you focus on yourself. Getting out Christmas tree ornaments one by one and decorating the tree can be a draining emotional experience when you are grieving. The temptation may be great to "forget it." But consider the importance of the Christmas tree and gifts to the children. A friend or relative will likely be more than happy to decorate your tree and help you purchase and wrap gifts.

Utilize Available Resources

Persons of religious faith are encouraged to utilize their church, synagogue, or other community of faith in coping. Some "veterans of faith" have serenity, a quiet presence and a healing wisdom. Seek them out for the support and wisdom their presence offers. You may wish also to seek out a support group of persons who have suffered similar losses. The Mental Health Association in most communities will have a list of available support groups. If one does not exist, establish your own short-term support group to help get through the holidays. The most valuable helper is usually someone who shares a common loss, one who understands something of what you're going through. Spend as much time as possible with the person(s) you love most.

Most important, remember that you can't change the past. You can take charge of the present, however. And you can shape the future. Total recovery may never come. But what you make of the ashes of your trauma is up to you.

Our Michael's birthday was December 22. He was killed on February 4, so that time is very emotional. The first Christmas of my married life was spent in the hospital with my own 'babe.' Now, six years later, we still hurt, but we go on.

Each December 22, Mike's brothers have a pizza party in his memory. When he would have been 22, nine of his friends got together on the 22nd and ate 22 pieces of pizza. What a marathon!

Rita Chiavacci

NOTES

X

<u>SPIRITUALITY</u>

"I no longer believe that God is a 'good' God."

"You'll never see me darken the door of a church again."

"Only my faith in God has enabled me to endure this."

"If one more person tells me that God needed another flower in his garden, I'm going to throw up."

All of these are common spiritual reactions to victimization. About one-third of victims say their experience strengthened their faith. Another third say the victimization did not change their faith. And one-third say their faith was diminished. Many victims say their personal faith became stronger but their connection to their church or synagogue weakened.

Even if you rarely thought about God before your loved one was killed, you have probably contemplated God in relation to death.

A minister, priest, or rabbi may have officiated at the funeral of your loved one. You may have received faith-oriented sympathy cards. Friends and relatives may have attempted to comfort you with references to God. When death comes, like it or not, most families deal with "God."

Some people experience God as a personal supporter, a presence bigger than life who gives them strength and peace. They say that their faith in God sustains them as they endure their suffering.

Most survivors are confused by God's apparent lack of intervention and may become angry with God. They believe that they were faithful religious people and God let them down by allowing their loved one to be killed.

"I feel so bad. I just can't comprehend it, it's so horrible," I wrote three months after John was killed. All I can say is "Oh my God, Oh my God." I feel like I'm going to split into pieces. Why did God let this happen? If there's a God, I hate Him.

Margaret Grogan,
whose son was murdered

Others feel their faith remains strong, but are confused and frustrated with the things people say about God. They wonder why, in the midst of staring death in the face, anyone would dare talk about "eternal life" or "heaven" as if that should take all the tears away.

Friends, relatives, and even the clergy sometimes say religious things that can hurt more than help. Almost always, these people mean well. They want to help you feel better. They may not know how. Or, more likely, they may not understand that feeling better is probably not possible for you for some time, and that all you really want is for them to join you in your suffering.

Chapter 10

It is also possible that you might misunderstand what others mean when they talk about God.

I rarely attended church before Adrianne was killed. However, the church I belonged to supported me more than I could possibly have imagined. Sometimes people said insensitive things, but I knew they were trying. I found my basic faith getting stronger. I don't think I could have survived without feeling God was with me.

Linda Jones, whose daughter
was murdered

Linda Jones was able to see past the inappropriateness of some of the things said to her and accept the physical manifestations of their care for her and her family.

"It Was God's Will"

This "consolation" may bring more pain and anger to family members than any other well-intended phrase. A sudden, violent death is absurd. Your loved one didn't deserve it. You don't deserve it. Therefore, for God to have willed it makes no sense.

In your pain, you may cry out, "Why? Why?" even though you understand the cause of the killing. You long for a better explanation — a deeper, more profound reason.

It is paradoxical that the more you long for an answer to the mysterious "why," the more difficult it seems to find answers. The cause of a tragic death is usually someone's choice or negligence. It is a "human being" problem rather than a "God" problem. As long as humans have the freedom to make choices, some will choose to be evil at worst, negligent at best, and the innocent will suffer the consequences.

Into the midst of your turmoil about the "why," a

well-meaning person may tell you that the tragedy was "God's will." Such a person implies that a mystical reason was responsible for your loved one's death, and the reason is known only by God. They imply that the reason is beyond understanding. Only you can decide if that reasoning makes sense.

If this line of reasoning doesn't make sense and is unacceptable, you will probably feel angry and resentful about the explanation. You may identify with the Jewish leader who responded, "Oh, I hope not," when asked if there was a meaning to the holocaust.

Why, then, do people so often use the phrase, "It was God's will?" It is an easy answer to a question they don't understand.

Persons who relate to you after the killing of your loved one are usually nervous and anxious. They want to be helpful. They want you to feel better, but they may not think before speaking.

When a child asks, "Why is the grass green?" it's easy to respond, "That's the way God made it." When the grass turns brown and looks dead, it's easy to give the same response. It quiets the child and provides an escape for the parent who may not have a scientific answer to the question.

God's role in what happened to you is your own faith decision. If you believe that somehow it was "God's will" that's fine. If it doesn't make sense, try to understand that those who say it mean well. They may be sharing their own faith decision and are not trying to hurt you. They want you to believe that God still provides for you and cares for you.

Chapter 10

"It's Sinful to be Angry"

Perhaps you grew up being told that it was bad to feel or display anger. Just as Santa Claus or the Easter bunny might not come if you were "bad" or acted angry, so would God reject you if you felt angry.

It is amazing that so many people believe that anger is bad when most religions address anger as a significant component in fighting or counteracting evil. Why then are some people so eager to tell you piously that you should not be angry?

Probably because they fear you might do violent deeds because of your anger. The thought of a suicide or homicide on your part, in response to the killing of your loved one, would be the ultimate trauma to those who love you. They would feel better if you assured them that you will not make irrational decisions. Feeling rage, revenge, or fantasizing about "doing in" the offender does not mean you are a vigilante or will act on your feelings.

It is extremely rare that persons deeply in grief make serious plans to kill the offender. They may think about it, but they very rarely commit a hostile or criminal act.

If your friends are so agitated about your anger that they feel compelled to try to stop your angry feelings, assure them that no harm will come to the offender or yourself. If you believe that the God of your faith can handle your anger, rage, thoughts about revenge, and confusion, tell them. You will feel better if you do, and so will they.

> *Help! I can't stand this anymore!*
> *Get me out of here, God!*
> *The mud of my distress*

Has sapped my strength,
Disrupted my belief,
Drowned my faith.
Where are you, God?

    Why won't you rescue me
From this mire?

"Move over.

I don't promise to remove you
from the pain of living.
But I do ask you to give me room
To sit in the mud beside you.

Remember my promise to never leave you?
Trust me.
Move over."

                    Dorothy Mercer

"You Must Forgive"

Without a doubt, you will be called upon to rethink your concept of forgiveness. In order to survive the trauma and stay healthy, you will need to decide how to deal with the offender and maintain your integrity.

In killings in which the offender was also killed, the issue of forgiveness can be avoided somewhat. For those in which the offender is alive, especially if the criminal justice system is involved in the case, the issue cannot be avoided.

Society tends to forgive easily. It is so eager to forgive that it doesn't require remorse on the part of the offender. Many homicides are plea-bargained in the criminal justice system with the offender being advised by their attorney to plead guilty to a lesser offense in return for a more lenient sentence. At the same time, the offender is instructed not to make contact with family members of the victim because it might imply an admission of guilt. Does society and the criminal justice system really believe that such a plea is genuine remorse? Apparently so. It is all that is required.

Your family may say, "If only he would look me in the eye and genuinely say `I'm sorry,' it would mean all the world to me." The common response to such a statement is that "only a vengeful family would put an offender through that." To you it may be a very significant component in justice with integrity.

Some family members of the victim have offered forgiveness when shown genuine remorse by an offender, even though they can never forget. Many more, however, cannot forgive. Most are unwilling to offer a "cheap grace" to offenders, a gesture of forgiveness that has no real meaning because the offender has shown no remorse and has made no commitment to a change in behavior.

You will need to decide, based on your own life experiences and religious convictions, how you view forgiveness. It is a difficult task. If others imply that you should offer forgiveness, tell them it is an important matter, and that you will handle it in a manner compatible with your integrity.

Both the Hebrew scriptures and the New Testament of Christianity emphasize God's compassion for the abused and oppressed, not the oppressors. God opposes violence and supports it only in those cases where sin is rampant and sinners are unwilling to repent and change their ways _ such as in Sodom and Gomorra. Jesus did not always forgive. In fact, He said *"Who-*

ever causes one of these little ones ('followers' on the Greek)
who believe in me to sin, it would be better for him if a great
millstone were hung around his neck and he were thrown into
the sea. '(Mark 9:42) Clearly, God stands with the sufferer.

Judith Herman, noted trauma counselor and researcher,
has pointed out in her book, Trauma and Recovery, that both
revenge and forgiveness can derive from attempts at empowerment. It is easy to understand vengeance as empowerment, even
though the consequences of acting it out would likely enhance
the powerlessness. It is a little more complicated to think of forgiveness that way. The idea in its simplistic form, however, is
that forgiving the offender will transcend the rage and erase the
impact of the trauma. It is seen as a willed, positive act while
vengeance is a willed, negative act. The myth is that one or the
other will remove pain. Obviously, neither an act of hatred nor of
love can fully transcend the trauma. Both are relational _ neither
can be accomplished in isolation.

Love is unconditional. Forgiveness is not. Some say that
forgiveness is divine. However, in nearly all religions, including
Christianity and Judaism, forgiveness is not unconditional. Even
a Japanese proverb points out that "Forgiving the unrepentant is
like drawing pictures in the water." It is not an easy, simple one-
time quick fix. It is a complex theological issue and it is not to be
granted until the offender has sought it and earned it through con-
fession, repentance, and restitution.

It may be useful for you to realize that most references to
forgiveness in the Bible are between God and a person. A relationship that was broken became restored. Jesus does not forgive
the strangers gambling for his clothing at the foot of the cross.
He asks God to, perhaps knowing that they have abandoned their
relationship with God. Even in the stories of human forgiveness
in the Bible, it is not granted simply at a whim. The father in the

parable of the prodigal son does not go looking for his son to offer him forgiveness while he is spending the family inheritance on wine, women, and song. It is only when the son realizes the foolishness of his ways and comes home, tells his father that he is sorry and plans to change his ways, that the father embraces him and plans a welcoming party. Forgiveness leads to reconciliation of two people who originally loved each other and then fell out of relationship. Most family members of someone murdered never had a relationship with the offender in the first place, so what is there to be restored?

Psychological and theological issues are both at stake in what people call forgiveness. The word has different meanings for different people. Many use the word "forgiveness" when what they describe is a psychological "letting go." It is unilateral.

An example of psychological letting go is Betty Jane Spencer, who has been quoted several times in this book. For years after her four sons were murdered, she was filled with rage for the offenders and for God. Through counseling, she was able to restore herself to and re-enter a relationship with God. She could set aside or let go of her rage toward the offenders, although she remains cautious because they have said their only regret is that they did not kill her that night, too. Forgiveness, in the theological sense, does not seem right to her because it implies a willingness to mutually enter a relationship with the offenders. She did not have a relationship with them before they murdered her family, and she has no desire to enter one now. If they wish to restore their broken relationship with God, she is more than happy for them to do so. In the meantime, she no longer harbors negative feelings for them that might be detrimental to her.

David Augsburger, noted theologian and author of *Helping People Forgive*, further describes the mutual or bilateral nature of forgiveness as "experiencing healing and well-being by regaining the other as a brother or sister; celebrating restored or recreated relationships."

An example of bilateral forgiveness is Elizabeth Menkin, whose sister, Elaine, was killed by Suzana Cooper while driving drunk. Elizabeth was filled with rage until the day she and her young niece went to look at the wrecked cars. Her niece noted that there were children's toys in the offender's minivan. They realized that the young woman who had killed their sister and aunt was a mother. Over the following weeks, Elizabeth Menkin's thoughts, as well as her father's, returned to the children whose mother was now in prison. They began to feel as if they had a relationship with the children, and vicariously, to their young mother. At that point, they sought out a victim-offender program in Oregon to begin preparation to meet with Suzana.

As she struggled with thoughts of the meeting, Elizabeth Menkin pondered her Jewish faith and the "R's" of Yom Kippur: Recognition of having sinned, Remorse, Repentance, Restitution, and Reform. She could not offer Suzana Cooper forgiveness without evidence of these things on Suzana's part; these were the things she believed God required of her for her own forgiveness. Elizabeth became clear that forgiveness did not have to be given, but it could be earned. She thought she could do it if it were earned.

Recognition, remorse, and repentance were clear upon their first meeting when Suzana could barely speak through her tears. Eventually, she accomplished the remaining two tasks as she entered a relationship with the Menkin family. During her 19 months in prison, Suzana was required to write to her own children every week and to write to the victim's family quarterly, reporting on her progress. She was ordered to attend parenting classes and alcoholics anonymous meetings in prison, and to ob-

tain her General Equivalency Degree (GED). When she was released, she was ordered to donate 10 percent of her earnings to
charity, to go to church with her children, and to work to get
other drunk drivers off the road. Nearly two years after Suzana's
release, she was still doing well.

"Now all I hope is that Suzana will eventually be able to
view herself not as someone who did a terrible thing, but as one
who, having made a terrible mistake, is now doing a courageous
and honorable thing," says Elizabeth Menkin.

If you are considering forgiveness, consider it seriously.
Theologian Dietrich Bonhoffer says that to do otherwise is to
offer "cheap grace." Take your time and make it the right decision for yourself, your family, and the offender. The right decision is the one that stems from your personal integrity and faith.
This decision may or may not be one that someone else feels is
best for you.

"If You Just 'Turn It Over to God,' You'll Be All Right"

Some may suggest that God is like a tranquilizer who
will smooth the rough edges if you have enough faith. To make
such a difficult task sound so simple may irritate you. Perhaps
you have prayed, but your prayers did not seem to be answered.
Or you may have prayed and found a sense of calm and peace,
but you are still confused. Veterans of faith in most religions find
something of an "abiding presence" in the midst of their longing
and suffering. They experience their God not so much as a solution to their problem of grief, but as a Companion who stands
with them in the midst of it. That kind of faith gives strength.

Because most of the people who love you feel inadequate
to help you feel better, they wish that God would do it for them.
They especially wish that their God would be present in you.

144

Thus, words that may sound overly simplistic and trite actually may be expressions of their own genuine concern and love.

You may or may not believe that the soul of your loved one lives on in eternity. If you do, that, in itself, is consoling. It does not mean, however, that you do not have the right to miss and deeply long for the body and presence that you no longer can see, hear, or touch. Perhaps it will be helpful to you, as well as those who attempt to comfort you, to explain that there are many components of grieving and that you are dealing with the religious components as honestly as you can. For example, you may find that after months or years, when you reach out to others you will find some of the answers.

> *Recently I asked Elie Wiesel how to overcome despair. We had been talking about things touching on despair, and on God. Hence my question. This man, who, more than most, has reason to despair, this man who lost his family in the death camp and himself barely survived, looked at me with those deep, dark eyes that have looked into the abyss and said, "You want to know how to overcome despair. I will tell you. By helping others overcome despair."*
>
> *He waited, then smiled a small smile. I realized the truth of what he'd said because I was feeling less despair in that moment precisely because he and I had talked together, shared together our struggles. He was saying that in that, I had helped him with his despair even as he helped me with mine. Eternal life and whatever hints at it is something we cannot have alone, only together.*
>
> *Theodore Loder, Pastor,*
> *FirstUnitedMethodist*
> *Church of Germantown,*
> *Philadelphia*

Chapter 10
After-Death Spiritual Experiences

Mystical experiences are fairly common among those whose loved one has died. They can be very spiritually and emotionally healing to those fortunate enough to have them.

Loved ones frequently report receiving direct and spontaneous communication from the deceased family member. These communications range from a vague sense of the deceased person's presence to hearing voices, seeing visions (transparent figures to full bodies), feeling touches, and smelling aromas such as the loved one's perfume or after-shave. Verbal or unspoken communications frequently center on "I'm okay," "Don't grieve for me," "I love you," or a derivative of "Goodbye."

No one knows for sure if these reported occurrences are true messages from the deceased or merely a coincidence that was assigned meaning for the comfort of the receiver. It is clear, though, that they offer reassurance and comfort to surviving loved ones.

Don't be surprised at very vivid dreams. I believe that Adrianne comes to me this way when she knows I need comfort. I think they come back to us, especially after a violent death because so much is unresolved. They are just "there"_ there's no doubt about it. As time goes on and as I become more healed, Adrianne's visits aren't as frequent or intense. I think she knows that if she didn't back out slowly and sweetly, it would be harder for me to go ahead and heal.

Linda Jones, whose daughter
was murdered with a gun

If you have had such an experience, accept it and celebrate it in whatever way you find meaningful. Share it with a few people you can trust. You will probably be surprised at the number of people who have had similar experiences.

This phenomenon is discussed openly in many cultures of the world. Our society is so scientifically oriented that we easily lose touch with the mystical.

On the other hand, try not to despair if you have not had this kind of experience. No one knows why some do and others do not. It is probably unwise to seek out "psychics" to try to force this experience or to solve the crime. Some are legitimate, but many are not.

All of these issues of faith are an important part of your grief process. Processing them takes time and effort. By engaging them, you can feel satisfied that you are working through the spiritual component of your loss, which also affects the emotional component. It is hard work.

Suggestions:

Following are some guidelines for dealing with the spiritual dimensions of your suffering.

- Look for someone who has had an experience similar to yours who also has a meaningful faith. If you feel comfortable doing so, ask that person how their faith is helpful to them. You may or may not be able to share their experience.

- Avoid discussion with people who use God as a simple answer to complex questions. Try to accept the fact that their faith journey may have been different from yours.

- Avoid conflict with people who are not comfortable with your anger and range of feelings. Assure them that you will not harm yourself or others as a result of your feelings.

- Try reading a few chapters from the Book of Psalms in the Bible, perhaps Psalms 23 and 139. Write in a journal or notebook what they mean to you.

- Think seriously about forgiveness and what you desire for it to mean to you and to the offender. Do not let anyone force you to say words you do not mean.

- If you continue to be troubled about religious feelings or beliefs, contact a hospital chaplain or a counselor of your religion. These people have had special training in accepting and dealing with traumatic grief. Or you can seek out a pastor, priest or rabbi who has previously been helpful to you or others.

XI

PROFESSIONAL COUNSELING

It is not easy to decide if or when you need the help of a professional counselor to cope with your grief. Many people find counseling is helpful, even if they feel they could get along without it. Counseling certainly will not hurt you if your counselor has some understanding of trauma following the killing of a loved one and is committed to treating survivors with dignity and compassion.

As previously discussed, traumatic grief has many of the same symptoms as clinical depression:

- Appetite changes

- Sleep disturbances

- Physical complaints

- Decreased sexual desire

- Loss of energy

- Inability to concentrate

• Need to withdraw

These normal symptoms of grief following tragic loss can be misdiagnosed if the counselor is not fully aware of what you have experienced. These symptoms may be relieved somewhat with small doses of antidepressants. If you take them, expect several weeks to pass before you feel their effect.

Over the years, additional symptoms have been identified that commonly occur in trauma survivors. Symptoms include:

• Unanticipated periods of crying (grief spasms) that can recur for years

• Occasional dreams and flashbacks

• Anger that is difficult to focus

• Difficulty deciding what to do with mementos, clothing and other possessions of the deceased

• Deep sadness, including irrational death wishes such as homicidal or suicidal fantasies

• Fear and anxiety, particularly about getting out in the community alone.

These symptoms should be considered normal after a traumatic loss. It is rarely, if ever, appropriate to look at grief from the medical model, i.e., "You are sick and therefore require treatment to get well again." It is more appropriate to look at the severity of the trauma that caused the symptoms, and then decide if they are normal reactions to a very abnormal event.

No one knows for sure how long you should grieve, how

many symptoms you should expect, or how intense a particular symptom will be for you. We do know that for most people, the grieving is painful and it lasts a long time.

It is even difficult to label your progress as you move through grief and begin to feel better. "Recovery" sounds like you were sick and became well again. Very few people who have had someone they love killed ever feel completely "recovered." Most say they are changed by their loss. ``Healing" is rarely complete. You will, however, feel better over time.

Many survivors rejuvenate on their own if they have family and friends who accept them, support them, and join them in their grieving. You will need to talk about the circumstances of the death, and to share memories of your loved one over and over again. It is a way of coming to grips with your loss.

Supportive family and friends can play a major role in your improvement. If they are unable or unwilling, you can find support from organizations that provide grief support groups. Many survivors spend months or years in a support group as they regain emotional health. If a group is not available, or you find a group does not help, you may decide to seek professional help. Some choose professional help along with support groups.

Most people know when they need professional help. They know because their physical symptoms are severe or because they are not improving. Some know they need help because their emotional pain is too difficult to endure. A professional counselor can help you assess your thoughts and feelings to determine if they are appropriate to your loss and grief. It is paradoxical that sometimes when you are feeling unsure, you are actually progressing well through your grief.

The remainder of this chapter can serve as a checklist as you contemplate the help of a professional counselor. Following are some of the symptoms that indicate you may need counseling and/or short-term prescription medication to help you to feel better. After a period of professional help, you may find that friends, family, and/or a support group are sufficient.

Getting "Stuck" in Grief

Grieving the loss of a loved one to a violent and unanticipated death continues, to some degree, for years. But if you look over the last several months or years and see that your grief is just as intense now as it was after the tragedy occurred, you may be "stuck." The pain of having a loved one killed takes awhile to surface. It is more intense and lasts longer than the pain of most anticipated and non-violent deaths. If you cannot look back and see that you are getting better, or you cannot imagine ever feeling better in the future, you may need professional help.

Absence of Grief

It is true that not all people grieve openly. Some people seem able to take trauma in stride. They may carry on, busy and efficient, and appear to be coping well. It is wise, however, if you are one of these people, to look carefully and sensitively at yourself. Do you feel anxious when you think of the one who was killed? Are you uncomfortable when friends offer sympathy? Do you forbid others to talk about your deceased loved one? Are you more tense and short-tempered than you were before?

Nearly all people grieving the killing of a loved one go through a period of denial when nothing about the death seems real. That is normal. In time, reality sinks in. Though difficult, it is healthy to lean into the pain and not fight it.

You may be afraid to think about your dead loved one because you think the pain will be intolerable. You may fear losing control. If you are "carrying on as usual," but find that it

Professional Counseling takes a lot of energy to keep yourself from thinking about your dead loved one or to keep others from reminding you, you may need the help of a professional in facing your grief and loss. Failure to get help can manifest itself in emotional withdrawal from the people you love or in physical illness.

Pre-existing Problems

If you had problems coping with your life before your loved one was killed, it is likely that those problems will increase. Health problems may get worse. If you have a history of mental or emotional problems, they may get worse. If your family or your marriage suffered problems, they may get worse. If you were a "loner" and didn't attract people to support you before, you will probably have difficulty finding support now.

Sudden death in a dysfunctional family can be complex. Families in which members abuse alcohol or other drugs, families in which physical or sexual abuse are common, and even families in which one or both parents are workaholics are families in which denial reigns as a style of life. People pretend that what's going on is not really happening. In most cases, these adults suffered deep emotional trauma as children. They learned to deny the pain in order to cope. They learned to pretend. In fact, the worse things were at home, the better they looked and acted in public.

These unspoken rules, "Don't feel what you feel," "Don't talk about your pain," "What happens in the family is the family's business and no one else's," can be extremely detrimental in acknowledging and leaning into grief. For many, a courageous and painful journey back to childhood will be required before the present grief can be faced. Under stress, most people resort to their lowest level of functioning. Members of a dysfunctional family are adept at appearing to stay in control in order to cover up the pain. That is exactly the opposite of what is required for grief work.

These facts need not discourage you. They simply mean that if you had problems in your family before the death, you are more likely than others who do not have these factors in their lives to need professional help. You must take responsibility to seek the help you and your family need.

Negative Self-Concept

Self-esteem can suffer when sudden violent death invades a family. Many survivors feel guilty and blame themselves for what happened. Most feel inadequate in trying to comfort others. Most wonder if they are strong enough to survive their grieving.

In time, however, rational thinking returns and survivors are able to place responsibility appropriately. If you are unable to return to rational thinking; if you feel that you are bad, incompetent, and to blame; you probably need to talk these perceptions through with a professional counselor. Negative self-concepts and grief are a formidable combination, especially when they continue beyond normal expectations. You deserve help in coming to grips with them.

Excessive Guilt

Guilt, as noted previously, is normal for some time during the grief process. If your relationship with the one who was killed was good, you will likely be able to resolve your guilt in time. You will be able to remember the good times along with the bad times.
Longing and yearning for the person will still be a focus of your life, however.

On the other hand, if your relationship with the one who

was killed was troubled, guilt may consume you. It can be so devastating that your conscience shoves it underground and forgets the bad times. Then, the hostility is no longer felt and the one killed is placed on a pedestal. This phenomenon is common when a teenager or the parent of a teenager is killed. Negative feelings are common as adolescents break away from the family. This also may happen when one partner in a troubled marriage is killed.

Sometimes, the guilt can be so severe that the survivor keeps the victim mentally alive in order to cope. In such cases, the deceased is referred to as if he or she is still alive. Most survivors have nightmares and flashbacks from which they emerge wondering if the victim really is dead. That is normal. But the person needing professional help will believe, all the time, that their loved one is still alive.

Sometimes the survivor needs to believe he can continue to communicate with the deceased. He may devise magical rituals to communicate. It is normal for survivors to need time before they are able to sort through the clothing or dwelling of a loved one. But people deeply in distress sometimes make a "shrine" of the things their loved one possessed or the room or house in which he lived. This person insists the room be left exactly as it was before the loved one died, and becomes enraged if anyone attempts to move something. This survivor might attach magical significance to the room and touch certain things or look at particular objects as a means of seeking some kind of attachment to the deceased. A skilled counselor understands why a survivor finds it necessary to respond in this manner and will gently and patiently help the survivor to face both the good and the bad to grieve appropriately.

Chapter 11

Dependency

Losing someone upon whom you are dependent is extremely traumatic.

A child whose parent has been killed cannot easily transfer dependence to a new caretaker.

Losing a child can devastate an elderly parent who depends on his adult child for care.

The spouse who relies on the mate for physical care, instruction, comfort, and support will be filled with stress, fear, and anxiety when forced to go it alone.

Some parents depend heavily on their child to fulfill their needs. A mother can feel that she is important only because her child needs her. Obviously, she will have a very difficult time coping if her child is killed.

Social support from family members and friends, and a transfer of emotional and physical needs to others who can be trusted to meet these need is essential for a dependent survivor to get better. If these people are unavailable to you, find a professional counselor to help you find yourself again and learn a new way to live.

Suicide

Suicidal thoughts are not uncommon among the traumatically bereaved. As denial and shock give way to painful physical symptoms, deep anger, and great sadness, many survivors say they, too, long to die to escape the pain and/or to be reunited with their loved one. Most of them, however, will think rationally about the consequences of suicide and look for a more constructive way to cope. One mother's despair overcame her to the degree that she took a gun to her daughter's grave, planning to commit suicide. As she swept the fallen snow from the headstone, she became keenly aware that she did not believe she would ever see her daughter again in eternity if she killed herself.

If your despair goes beyond a desire to simply not wake up in the morning and you become pre-occupied with the idea of killing yourself, you must seek professional help. If you find yourself unable to think rationally, or if you have devised a plan for your own demise, you must tell someone. A counselor can help you find other ways to relieve the pain.

If you seriously contemplate suicide, you may find that your mind is focused on the one who is likely to discover your body. You may be angry with that person and contemplate using the suicide to hurt him or her. A counselor can help you discover other ways of handling that problem.

If you have made up your mind to commit suicide, it will take strength and courage on your part to change your mind. For the sake of those who love you, you must stop yourself until you have at least visited a counselor to help you consider other alternatives.

Finding a Good Counselor

It is sad but true that not all counselors or psychotherapists are skilled at grief therapy following a violent and unanticipated death. Therefore, you may need to shop around for the right counselor.

Word of mouth is the best referral source. Call the support groups in your community to find other survivors who can suggest potential counselors. There are many non-profit counseling and support groups such as Compassionate Friends, Parents of Murdered Children, The Bell Campaign, MADD, and

Mental Health agencies. They can provide support or give you referrals to grief counselors.

After obtaining counselor names, call several and ask the following questions:

1. Have you ever worked with clients who have had a loved one killed? How many?

2. What kind of counseling do you do with people deeply in grief?

3. Under what circumstances do you arrange for prescription drugs?

4. About how many sessions do you have with a client who is having problems with grief?

5. What licenses or certifications do you have?

6. How much continuing education have you received during the last few years? Have you had any training in grief therapy?

7. Do you provide individual counseling only or do you have victim support groups as well?

8. How much do you charge? Do you take insurance? Do you offer a sliding scale?

The most important rule in finding a professional counselor who can help you is to trust your "gut" feelings. If after two or three sessions you do not feel supported, understood and comfortable, you have the right to go elsewhere. You cannot get better in therapy unless you feel emotionally connected to the therapist in a way that makes you feel safe to share your thoughts and feelings honestly. Keep the following questions in mind throughout therapy:

- Do I sense that my therapist is competent to work with victims who are mourning sudden violent death?

- Do I feel that my therapist cares about me and recognizes my needs?

- Do I feel that I am making reasonable progress?

Therapy can be painful. A good counselor will support you as you work through the pain. You will find yourself looking forward to the sessions because you trust your counselor will treat you with dignity and compassion. If that does not happen, look elsewhere.

NOTES

XII

COPING WITH THE CRIMINAL JUSTICE SYSTEM

You may think that coming to grips emotionally with the killing of your loved one is your sole task. Unfortunately, it is not.

After most killings, the offender is apprehended. In some murders and in hit-and-run vehicular crashes, the offender is never found. This situation adds another component to the grieving of surviving family members and friends. The need for justice is totally thwarted in these cases and can result in more complicated grieving. It is difficult to focus anger when no one is clearly responsible. Feelings of helplessness and hopelessness can emerge. The anger can easily, if not always appropriately, be focused on law enforcement agencies who cannot locate the offender.

When the offender is also killed, survivors report mixed emotions. Some feel a sense of relief, although this does not diminish the grief for their loved one. Others believe the offender should have been punished by the criminal justice system.

If the offender was not killed and was apprehended, you likely will be thrust into the criminal justice system. It is against

Criminal Justice System
the law to kill someone, intentionally, maliciously, or with criminal negligence. Therefore, the State has a responsibility to prosecute the offender for the commission of a crime, and to attempt to obtain a conviction.

As the surviving family, you probably are interested in obtaining justice and seeing the offender punished, even though no sentence seems just or adequate for what was done to your loved one.

The word State is significant. Your family is not a party to the criminal suit. The legal document reads "The State v. Offender Name." It does not read "Victim Name v. Offender Name." Unless you were present when your loved one was killed and are an eyewitness to the offense, you will not automatically be involved in the case.

Most family members of the victim find the perceived detachment of criminal justice system personnel extremely frustrating. You may say, "It was not my State that was killed. It was my loved one!"

While that is true, it is the role of the State to punish the offender because he has broken the law. You will learn more about bringing a personal lawsuit against the offender (a civil lawsuit) in the next chapter.

I can accept a great deal of ignorance and a great deal of lack of awareness—but to be told that I am not a real victim when I have lost something that is more precious to me than my own life, I will not tolerate. If you feel you are not dealing with real victims when you deal with homicide survivors, just call me.

Dorothea Morefield,
whose son was murdered

Within the last few years, the criminal justice system has become more involved with the victim's family in most jurisdictions. A U.S. Supreme Court case has upheld the right of victims to testify about the impact of the crime on their lives. This generally happens during the sentencing portion of a trial, even in death penalty cases. Crime victim families now have statutory rights in all 50 states, although victims are still not a party to the criminal law suit.

While these statutes vary from state to state, they generally include the following:

- the right to protection from intimidation from the offender

- the right to be notified of all hearings in the criminal justice process (although you must tell the victim advocate or prosecutor that you want to be informed)

- the right to information about Crime Victim's Compensation and other victim's services

- the right to give the prosecutor your opinion about proposed plea bargains

- the right to be present and heard during the trial

- the right to present a written (and in many states an oral) Victim Impact Statement before the offender is sentenced

- the right to an order of restitution

- the right to be notified of probation and parole hearings

- the right to be notified of the release or escape of the

While these laws are in place, not all prosecutors or representatives of the State grant these rights to the victim family. Since many of these rights are on paper only, you may have to be assertive in order to claim them.

When my son was kidnapped, brutally beaten to death, and twice robbed, neither the law enforcement nor the justice system acknowledged the existence of survivors of homicide victims, let alone allowed them any rights.

Though such sloppy treatment is not as widespread today as it was then, there remains considerable, die-hard resistance to the rights of survivors, even in those states where legislation provides for them. There is little or no recourse to that resistance and no effective reprimands for those who "forget" to extend said rights.

Janet Barton

What Can You Do?

The Crime Report

The crime report is prepared by the law enforcement agency that investigated the killing of your loved one. It is usually the City Police Department if the crime happened within city limits. Generally, the County Sheriff's Department investigates crimes outside the city limits. The State Highway Patrol takes charge of the investigation of highway crashes that occur outside the city limit. Call the appropriate agency and ask how and when you can receive a copy of the crime report. Supplemental reports are filed as more investigation is conducted. Ask if, how, and when you may obtain copies of the supplemental reports. Do not expect to receive everything. Much of the information must remain confidential until the trial is over.

The investigating officer should give you the identification number of the report, called the offense report. You may
also request the badge number of the investigating officer. If you
do not get the offense number, or if you lose it, you can obtain
the report by providing the date and scene of the crime. Knowing
the offender's name is helpful, but not essential. Look the report
over closely for the following data:

- Do you see errors in the report? If so, report them immediately to the investigating officer whose name is at the bottom
  of the report. Even if they seem minor, they can be crucial to
  the court case.

- Are there any indications on the report that the offender had
  been drinking or using drugs when he killed your loved one?
  If so, determine if a Blood Alcohol Content (BAC) level is
  indicated on the crime report. Breath, blood, or urine testing
  shortly after the crime was committed usually determines
  BAC. If the tests were not performed, you have the right to
  know why they were not.

*These tests should be routinely given following automobile
crashes in which alcohol or other drugs were used or suspected.
Valid BAC testing can result in tougher penalties and sentences
for drunk drivers.*

Blood alcohol and drug testing is not as routinely given
in other homicide cases because of the usual lapse of time between committing the crime and apprehension of the offender. In
many states, the consumption of alcohol or other drugs before or
during the crime, is considered a mitigating circumstance that
may result in a more lenient sentence, if it is not a vehicular crime.

The Investigating Agency (Police, Sheriff, State Trooper)

- Ask what charges are being recommended, why they were selected, and what elements of proof will be necessary to expect a conviction.

- Ask when the investigating agency is likely to transfer the case to the prosecutor's office (sometimes referred to as the county attorney, district attorney, or state's attorney). Leave your name and phone number and ask to be notified when the case is transferred. If you have not heard from someone within a few days after a case was expected to be transferred, call to inquire about the status of the case.

- Ask if the investigating agency has a victim advocacy program. It is the victim advocate's role to keep you informed of the status of the case and to provide services you may need as a crime victim. Services include referrals to appropriate agencies, victim counseling, and assistance in applying to the State Victim Compensation Program for reimbursement of uninsured expenses resulting from the victimization.

- If you are not satisfied with the information the investigating officer or victim advocate has provided, ask to speak with the investigating officer's supervisor.

Evidence

You may assume that the investigating officers have collected all the evidence they need. However, it is wise to document everything about the crime at the time it comes to your attention. You may think you will remember all the facts, but documentation will ensure a good recollection of all details.

- Additional witnesses may come forth who were not interviewed by the investigating officer. If so, refer them to the investigating officer or to the prosecutor who will take their statement.

- Investigators probably took pictures at the crime scene and at the medical examiner's office. It is possible, however, that other pictures would be useful in both the criminal and civil case. A recent picture of your loved one before he or she was killed may be presented to the court prior to sentencing. It will personalize your loved one in the eyes of the court. If you take pictures after the crime was committed that you think may be helpful, have someone witness your actions. Sign and date the photos on the back, and ask the witness to do the same. Offer the photographs to the investigating officer or prosecutor.

- Ask for the return of any clothing or personal effects that belonged to your loved one. These items may be in the investigator's office, hospital, or the medical examiner's office. Some of the items may need to be retained for the trial, but you should be given those that are not essential to the case. Ask about the condition of these things before opening the container to look at them.

- Begin a record or log with receipts and bills of all financial expenditures involved in the killing of your loved one. These may include medical and funeral expenses, lost wages, fees for hiring a private investigator, and costs of professional counseling for family members. This information will be critical if the offender is found guilty and the judge orders him to pay restitution to your family. It is also necessary in filing for State Crime Victim's compensation, insurance benefits, and civil suits.

The Prosecutor
After the investigating officer has transferred the case to the county attorney, district attorney, or state attorney, determine which prosecutor has been assigned to your case. Information will be filed under the defendant's name. Let the prosecutor know that you want to be informed of what is happening during all stages of the criminal process. In most states, you will not be informed unless you specifically request this. Therefore, the prosecutor and/or the victim advocate should be notified in person or by phone of your desire to be informed. Keep a log of all your calls.

A follow-up letter should be mailed to both the prosecutor and the victim advocate stating:
- the name of the accused,
- your name, address, and phone number,
- your desire to be informed,
- the facts as you understand them about the case, and
- any feelings you have about bail for the accused, plea bargaining, or any other aspect of the case.

Ask to be informed if the prosecutor changes the charge from its intended recommendation.

Understand Charging
After reviewing the evidence in the case, the prosecutor may:

- Issue the criminal charges recommended by the investigating agency;

- Issue different, lesser, or additional charges; or

- Decide not to issue charges because of insufficient evidence.

In most states, one of two procedures will be used to determine whether probable cause or sufficient evidence exists to proceed to trial.

- A preliminary hearing may be held in which the prosecutor and possibly a few witnesses appear before the judge. If the judge determines that sufficient evidence exists, the accused will be scheduled for arraignment.

- A grand jury hearing is much the same as a preliminary hearing except the prosecutor presents evidence to a group of citizens rather than to a judge. Most grand juries are composed of citizens who serve for several months at a time. Grand jury proceedings are closed to the public (including the victim's family). The accused is not present while others testify. The accused may or may not be called to testify. If the grand jury determines that sufficient evidence exists, they hand down a true bill of indictment. If they do not think that sufficient evidence exists, the case is "no-billed." If indicted by the grand jury, the accused is then scheduled for arraignment.

Arraignment

At the arraignment, the accused appears personally before a judge who informs him of the charges pending against him and of his constitutional rights, including the right to a court-appointed defense attorney. The accused is now called the defendant and will enter a plea of guilty or not guilty.

The Defense Attorney

The attorney for the defendant or one of his investigators may phone, write or appear on your doorstep. Before you communicate with any attorney or investigator, confirm his identity. Ask who he represents. A defense attorney is not a district attorney even though he may refer to himself as a DA. The defense attorney represents the rights of the accused and clearly is not there to represent your rights as a victim.

You do not have to speak to the defense attorney or investigator unless you are subpoenaed to do so. Ask him to get the requested information from the prosecutor's office. The prosecutor will accompany you if you are subpoenaed to give a deposition (statement) under oath.

Bail or Bond Hearing

Sometimes bond is set at the arraignment. Sometimes it is set at a separate hearing. Bail or bond is an amount of money given to a court by the defendant in exchange for his release and his promise to appear in court. The defendant can usually post bond through a bonding company for about 15% of the actual amount of bond set. If the offender is known by the victim, it can be very important for a representative of the victim family to be present when bond is set. This representative can inform the court of relevant facts concerning the defendant's likelihood to flee. Additionally, a family representative can address any potential danger to the family if the defendant is released from jail. This information could result in a higher bond or refusal of bond for a dangerous offender.

Discovery/Preliminary Hearings

After arraignment, the prosecutor and the defense attorney will gather evidence to support their cases. If the defendant has been arraigned on charges you do not understand, ask the prosecutor to explain to you the elements that must be proven to obtain a conviction. Discuss the strengths and weaknesses of the case. If you understand these, you may be able to provide additional information that will be helpful to the prosecution of the case. You may know of additional witnesses or have ideas about beneficial evidence. The prosecutor should know that you support him in trying to convict the defendant on the highest charges that can be proven.

Continuances

Ask to be informed of pre-trial hearings including requests for continuances. Pre-trial hearings are open to the public (including you) even though attorneys usually tell you it is unnecessary for you to be there. Defense attorneys usually request numerous "continuances," or postponements, to "age the case." They know that the longer they can postpone the trial, the more likely the State will lose its witnesses, or witnesses' memories will fade. Be sure the prosecutor vigorously opposes unnecessary continuances at every opportunity.

In some states, the prosecutor may request a speedy trial on the basis of sensitivity to victims. (Defendants have a constitutional right to a speedy trial, but it is rarely in their interest to request it, especially if they have been released on bond.) In some states, the judge is required to state the reason for granting a continuance in the court record.

Continuances may be requested by the State or by the defense. They are often for legitimate reasons, such as work conflicts or the unavailability of witnesses. They do not necessarily mean that your case is being ignored.

Until the trial, you are constantly hitting a brick wall. The initial investigators treated us badly _ as if we were totally ignorant. You know the cops and prosecutors know things that they aren't telling you, and when that happens your imagination goes wild. Only when it's over can they be totally open with you. Now that I understand the reasons they had to withhold information, I would say it's a pretty good justice system. Our DAs were great in that they told us everything they could. When they can't tell you something, it's really important that they tell you why not.

*Linda Jones, whose daughter
was shot and killed*

Ask the prosecutor or victim advocate if you have the right to be informed of pre-trial hearings and to provide input during the hearing. If your state guarantees these rights, claim them. Do your best to see that your case is not disposed of without your knowledge.

Plea Bargaining/Sentence Bargaining

These terms refer to negotiations that take place between the prosecutor and the defense attorney. These negotiations may result in a plea to a lesser charge or to a particular sentence in exchange for a reduced sentence. Bargains are usually distasteful to victim families who feel that to "cut a deal" is to betray the significance of the killing of their loved one. This is not always true.

In some circumstances, plea or sentencing bargaining is beneficial. If the preliminary investigation was inadequate, the offender may have been arraigned on a charge the State cannot now prove. It is better to allow the defendant to plead guilty to a lesser charge and to be punished, than to go to trial and lose everything.

Many states require that the victim's family be informed if plea or sentence bargains are considered. A few states allow the victim's family the right of input into bargaining decisions. Know your rights and assert yourself in claiming them. It is very important that you be present if a plea is presented to the judge. It will remind him that both the victim and the defendant should be considered in the decision rendered.

Chapter 12
Victim Impact Statements

All states have enacted laws or procedures that allow family members of the victim to give a written or oral statement to the court about the impact of the crime on their lives. These statements are presented after the defendant has been convicted and before he or she is sentenced.

Most judges require the Adult Probation Department of their county to conduct a Pre-Sentence Investigation (PSI) on a defendant. The purpose of this investigation is to collect information before sentencing. A convicted offender may be sent to jail for a certain number of days, or to state prison for a few or many years. If the sentence is probated _ served outside jail or prison _ conditions of probation can vary widely. The defendant may or may not be required to pay fines to the State. He may or may not be required to pay restitution to the victim's family. He may or may not be required to attend counseling, or a number of other options probation officers may recommend.

Until recently, pre-sentence investigations focused solely on the offender. The victims' movement has succeeded in convincing many state legislatures that unless the victim's perspective also is presented, the court has not heard the whole story. The advent of Victims Impact Statements is a tangible result of this movement.

It is very important that Victim Impact Statements be prepared and presented to both the prosecutor and the probation department before a hearing to consider a plea bargain or sentence bargain. If the judge decides to accept a guilty plea, he may proceed immediately to sentencing. Therefore, it is essential that the judge have immediate access to the Victim Impact Statements.

Most states have a Victim Impact form that can be

requested from the prosecutor, probation department, or victim advocates. If not, simply write an explanation of the emotional and/or physical impact the killing of your loved one has had on your family in letter form. Include any financial impact this egregious act has had on you. Include medical expenses, funeral expenses, lost wages, and any medical or counseling expenses that you incurred as a result of the trauma. Documentation of these expenses can result in the defendant being ordered to reimburse you. If your state statute allows, you may also include your opinion about the defendant's sentence.

Victim Impact Statements are a wonderful opportunity_ the only time you can speak face to face with the offender who is, by then, a convicted criminal. Each of us thought carefully about what we wanted to say so we could stay calm and remind him of what he will remember every night when he goes to sleep.

Linda Jones whose daughter
was shot and killed

In preparing statements, be sure your information is accurate. Write from the heart about your pain, but try not to make bitter or disparaging remarks about the offender. Judgment of the defendant belongs to the judge or jury.

Going to Trial

If the defendant persists in pleading not guilty, the case will be set for trial. He has a constitutional right to choose whether he wants his case to be decided by a judge (bench trial) or a jury. In most jurisdictions, the State must accept the form requested by the defendant. Be prepared for numerous postponements even after a trial date has been set.

Chapter 12

If the defendant chooses a jury trial, jury selection may take days or weeks before the trial actually begins. Most surviving families want to attend the trial although they know it will be an emotionally draining experience. Because trials can take several weeks, victim families may have difficulty getting off work to attend. Several states have now realized that victims should have the right to attend the trials concerning their loved ones without penalty, much the same as employees who are called to serve jury duty. Inquire about such statutes from your victim advocate or prosecutor. If no statute exists in your state, explain to your employer why it is important for you to be at the trial.

You may be surprised to learn that the defense may try to prevent you from attending the trial. The defense attorney's goal is to minimize sympathy for the victim during the trial. The defense wants any sympathy to be focused on his client, the defendant.

A common tactic of the defense is to subpoena you as a potential witness, and then ask the judge to invoke the "gag rule," a rule stating that witnesses cannot listen to each other testify. Even though you may not be called to testify, you will, thereby, be kept out of the courtroom, never to be seen by the judge or jury. If you did not witness the crime and, therefore, would not testify until sentencing, ask the prosecutor to advocate that you be allowed in the courtroom.

Stephanie never let me down. I had to be there to be sure the court didn't let her down.

> Roberta Roper, whose
> daughter, a college senior,
> was murdered

I had to go. It was my responsibility to Andy and Pam.

It would be evidence of their having been alive and loved.

> *Louise Gilbert, whose son
> and daughter-in-law were
> murdered*

*I don't want to be at the trial, but I can't not be there. I
don't want revenge, but I do want justice. And I think that he
should get the maximum if he's found guilty.*

> *Tinka Bloedow, whose 14-
> year-old daughter was
> killed by a drunk driver*

*We wanted to be there because no one was there to
defend our daughter. The only picture the jury saw of Catina
was the morgue picture. They had no idea what kind of girl she
was. That's why it is so important that families be there,
because the victim is not there to answer.*

> *Michael Salarno, whose 18-
> year-old daughter, Catina
> was murdered*

Several states now allow victims (or victim's representatives and family members) to be present during the trial if they
are not going to testify. If they are scheduled to testify, they are
allowed to remain in the courtroom following their testimony.
One state even allows the victim to sit with the prosecutor at
counsel table, just as the defendant sits beside the defense attorney.

Some prosecutors worry that the victim's family may become emotionally upset during the trial and unduly prejudice the jury, providing grounds for a mistrial. Assure the prosecutor that you will respect appropriate courtroom demeanor if you desire to be present in the courtroom.

Be aware of these general courthouse guidelines:

- Do not discuss the case in the halls or restrooms. Your behavior out of the courtroom is as important as your behavior inside.

- Never speak to the judge or a juror, even if you encounter them in the hall or at lunch. They must remain bias-free as they hear the evidence.

- Prepare yourself for the emotional impact of hearing the defendant say "not guilty." Even though you know you would not be in a trial unless he was pleading "not guilty," many victims report a jarring emotional reaction when they actually hear the words. In many cases, these are the first words the family has heard the defendant speak.

- Expect to hear upsetting testimony. You may hear gruesome details for the first time. You may see photos you have never been shown before. You may also hear the defense attorney attempt to show that your loved one was responsible for his or her own death. He has an ethical responsibility to do all he can to represent his client's legal interests. Therefore, much of what is important to you may seem like gamesmanship for players who try to out maneuver each other in courtroom drama. It is up to the judge or jury to determine the truth.

- If you feel you may lose control of your emotions during the trial, leave the courtroom. Your demeanor in the courtroom must not be intended to influence the judge or jury.

- If you have questions or concerns during the trial, write them down and give them to the prosecutor or victim advocate. Don't whisper during the trial.

- Victim advocates from the prosecutor's office or from support groups such as Mothers Against Drunk Driving, The Bell Campaign, Parents of Murdered Children, or Compassionate Friends are usually available at your request to attend court proceedings with you and answer questions at appropriate breaks.

The courtroom was a battlefield with combat played out between lawyers and a judge with a calm defendant dressed in his best.

> Louise Gilbert, whose son
> and daughter-in-law were
> murdered

It was a nightmare, an absolute nightmare. When you learn of the death, you go into shock. At the trial, reality sets in. But I still feel strongly that the family needs to be there.

> Harriet Salarno, whose
> 18-year-old daughter was
> murdered

Finally, after a number of postponements, we sat in the small *courtroom. I met the prosecutor and moments later came face to face with the man charged with killing my children. During the trial, I learned the meaning of horror, and their last hours were never again to leave my mind. Pam's fractured head and almost nude body were described in detail as well as the maggots and flies that covered her. I bolted the courtroom when the pathologist began to describe my son's bloated body.*

Louise Gilbert, whose son
and daughter-in-law were
murdered

Courtroom Procedure

Standard courtroom procedure during a criminal trial is as follows:

- Both attorneys give opening statements.

- The State calls witnesses to the stand in an attempt to prove that the defendant is guilty as charged. The prosecutor's questioning of each State witness is called "direct examination." The witness is then "cross-examined" by the defense attorney. The procedural rules for cross-examination are more liberal than rules for direct-examination. For example, in cross-examination, leading questions may be asked such as "Isn't it true that....?" After cross-examination, the witness is given "re-direct examination" by the prosecutor and "re-cross examination" by the defense. The witness is then dismissed, unless either attorney plans to call the witness back to testify later. Once dismissed, witnesses may usually remain in the courtroom. However, it is prudent to sit near the back of the courtroom out of the direct view of the judge or jury.

- After the State has presented all its witnesses, the defense will present its witnesses, going through the same procedures of direct and cross-examinations.

- After all the evidence has been presented, each side may introduce witnesses to rebut previously given testimony. Rebuttal witnesses can be witnesses who have previously testified but have not been dismissed, or they can be new witnesses.

- Each side presents closing arguments. The State has the burden of proof in the case and therefore has the right to argue both before and after the defense. Typically, the prosecutor will summarize the evidence before the defense argues. Then the prosecutor will rebut the defense's arguments.

- The judge gives the jury instructions for their deliberations, or if it is a bench trial, retires to deliberate himself.

The Verdict

Hearing the announcement of the verdict is the climax of the trial and is usually a very emotionally-laden time for the victim's family. You must be aware that a legal verdict and the truth are, unfortunately, not always the same. While a defendant may not, in truth, be innocent, he may be proven "not guilty." Judges and juries are the best way our society knows to determine legal justice. Judges and juries are also susceptible to human error. All of this must be kept in perspective.

The standard of proof in criminal cases is "beyond a reasonable doubt," the highest burden of proof required in any trial proceeding. This term is legally undefined. However, if any doubt based on reason exists as to any element of the offense as charged, the verdict of the judge or jury must be "not guilty." Evidence must establish the facts so clearly, positively, and explicitly that there can be no reasonable doubt that the case was proven.

Sentencing Trial or Hearing

If the defendant is convicted, the case will proceed to sentencing. Sentencing may occur immediately following the conviction or be scheduled for a later date. Even though you did not witness the crime, you may be allowed to testify during the sentencing hearing.

Written Victim Impact Statements are submitted to the prosecutor and probation departments before sentencing. A representative of these departments pass the statements on to the judge for consideration in sentencing. If oral impact statements are allowed in your jurisdiction, you may be called to the witness stand to testify about the impact of the crime on your life.

The prosecutor put me on the stand. He wanted the jury to hear first-hand about the devastating effect the killing of Stephanie had on our family. Defense objected. After a brief conference, the Judge agreed with the defense that legally, Stephanie's character and our grief were irrelevant.

I had been silenced. Yet, the defendant's former teacher and his prison minister would both speak on the defendant's behalf. The court deemed their statements relevant. I burned with anger.

Roberta Roper, whose daughter was murdered and who later introduced legislation, now law in Maryland, that Victim Impact Statements must be heard. The right has now been upheld by the U.S. Supreme Court

Evidence and procedures differ during sentencing _ sometimes called the dispositional phase of the trial. Defense witnesses will be called to provide subjective testimony about the defendant and why they feel he should receive a particular sentence.

Since the goal of your Victim Impact Statement is to convey the effect your loved one's killing has had on you, it is not expected that you testify free of emotion. Be aware, however, that judges and juries can tell the difference between genuine and contrived emotion.

You need not fear testifying if you have discussed your testimony honestly with the prosecutor and have thought through how you want to present it.

Following are some suggestions that should help you testify with relative ease and maximum credibility:

- Dress conservatively. Wear a business suit if you are a man, or a dress or business suit if you are a woman. Your clothing should not be flashy or in any way detract from what you are saying.

- Take notes or a written statement with you to the witness stand if you think you may need them. However, be aware that the judge, attorneys, and jury may be allowed to examine them.

- If the defense attorney asks if you have discussed your testimony with your attorney, it is appropriate to respond "yes." Your attorney may have helped you organize your statement, but you are testifying to the true impact of the killing on you and your family.

- If you don't understand a question by one of the attorneys, simply say so and ask that it be repeated. If you do not know the answer to a question, say so. If you feel an attorney is trying to manipulate you into an answer that is not true, turn to the judge and tell him that you will need to explain your answer.

- Be descriptive as you speak of the impact of the killing. Describe particular events that were/are painful for you. Your goal is to enable the judge or jury to come as close as possible to understanding how you felt when it happened and how you feel now.

- Do not use jargon or judgmental words if you say anything about the offender. Words such as "drunk," "alcoholic" and "crazy" are judgmental words you should not use. Talk about your pain and avoid bitter or disparaging remarks about the defendant.

- Avoid unnecessary phrases or cliches such as "I honestly believe that...." or " I can truthfully say that...." They are less powerful than short, simple statements.

- Maintain eye contact with the attorney who asks you the question. Don't look to your own attorney for help when being questioned by the defense attorney. Look at the judge or jury only if the attorney asks you to explain something to them.

- If you request that the defendant pay restitution to your family, be prepared to present actual bills and statements of the amounts paid or owed.

- Always be honest. Take your time. Pauses before your answers indicate that you are taking the question seriously and thinking before you speak. If you approach the task of testifying with integrity, your testimony will be respected.

Appeals

Following a conviction and sentencing, the defendant has a right to appeal the findings of the case to a higher court, and to ask for review of errors in procedure or application of the law at the trial court level. Be prepared for this phase, especially if the sentence is maximal. Many convicted felons are released on appeal bonds until the appeal is heard, which may be several years later. Under the concept of "innocent until proven guilty," a trial court decision is not considered final until appeals are heard. While this hardly appears fair from the victim's perspective, it is a procedural safeguard that has proven useful, especially when a convicted defendant is innocent.

Parole

Sentences assessed are seldom sentences served. Primarily because of prison overcrowding, the concept of "good time," credit given for days of imprisonment because of good behavior, is common. The convicted criminal may actually receive two or three more days' credit for each day served, and in fact, serves only a fraction of the actual sentence imposed.

Judge Haile gave Jones a life sentence for murder, a life sentence for rape, and twenty years for kidnapping. But, surprising even the defense, he announced that the sentences could be served concurrently. This meant that Jones would be eligible for parole in less than twelve years with credit for time already served and credit for good behavior.

Roberta Roper, whose
daughter was murdered

The boy who killed our daughter was a juvenile (17). He was found guilty of criminal negligence involving a death, drunken driving, and hit and run. He was sentenced to 90 days

Chapter 12

in a chemical dependency treatment and behavior modification program, his license suspended for six months, and he was placed on probation until his nineteenth birthday.

I later learned that he was again charged with drunk driving when he was twenty-one. The previous conviction had not been reported to the Public Safety Department and the new charge was being treated as a first time misdemeanor. When I finally got them to look into it, I learned that within six months of his license being reinstated, he had two speeding violations and another for driving with an open bottle. We got his license suspended again, but when the suspension was over, he was cited for an illegal turn and use of a motor vehicle in commission of a felony. Following yet another license revocation, he was cited with refusing a breathalyzer test following a drunk driving arrest. I'm enraged, absolutely enraged. I thought the system worked, but I'm not so sure now.

Tinka Bloedow, whose
daughter was killed by a
drunk driver

As soon as the convicted offender is placed in jail or prison, call to obtain his identification number. Include the personal identification number (PIN) and his full name in all correspondence with parole boards. Always include your own name and address so you can receive a response.

Send a copy of your original Victim Impact Statement to the Parole Board. Write the parole commissioners responsible for the particular facility to which the prisoner is assigned as well as the State Parole Board. Inform the Parole Board in writing from time to time about the ongoing impact of the death of your loved one. Especially send new letters when it is time for parole

Criminal Justice System
review. Petitions submitted requesting continuing incarceration are often impactful at review time. Call prior to the review and ask if you may provide an oral statement. In any event, leave your phone number and ask to be informed when the review decision is made.

Cases Against Juveniles

In most states, juvenile hearings are not open to the public, including the victim's family. Juvenile case files are closed. With increased frequency, however, victims of juvenile offenders have the same rights as victims of adult offenders.

Other Resources
Writing Letters

Letter writing should follow every interaction you have with the criminal justice system. Since a conversation may be forgotten, undocumented, or misconstrued, it is always wise to write a letter. It can prevent a prosecutor, probation, or parole officer from saying "I don't remember you saying..." or "I was never informed."

The League of Women Voters suggests that as you think about your letter, you consider the sentence, "_____ wants you to _____ because _____." Consolidating your concerns into this format will help you keep your letters clear and persuasive. Use short sentences and short paragraphs. Use action verbs such as "urge" rather than "wish" Be polite and respectful.

Never write a letter to the judge until the offender has been found guilty. Victim Impact Statements go to the prosecutor and probation department, who will present them to the judge at the appropriate time for the sentencing hearing or trial.

The Media

If the killing of your loved one was sensational, or if the criminal case is unique, the media may be eager to present it in written or broadcast form. It is your right to choose whether to speak with the media. If you decide to do so, it is best to contact your attorney first. You don't want to jeopardize your case in any way. Sometimes, excessive publicity can result in a change of location — or venue—for the trial.

If you speak with the media, be certain that you have your facts straight and that you refer to the defendant as the "accused" or "alleged criminal" until conviction. If you speak to a print media reporter, ask him to call and read the article to you before it goes to print so that necessary corrections can be made.

Remember: It is always your right to turn down an interview with the media or refer reporters who have questions to the attorney who is handling your case. Avoiding media questions until after the trial is often the best policy.

You may seek out a victim advocate who has media expertise to serve as your spokesperson or media representative. Once acquired, simply put a message on your answering machine indicating that all media calls are to be directed to that person. Use Caller ID and do not pick up the telephone. Your media representative will screen the calls and will call you only when necessary to see if you choose to respond to any inquires. If so, he or she will help you draft a response. Your prosecutor's victim advocate can help you locate a spokesperson.

Ethical Review Procedures

While the caliber of attorneys in a typical prosecutor's office is high, review procedures are available in most jurisdictions to investigate the conduct of individuals if you feel they have been unethical in the treatment of your case.

Most states have a Prosecutor's Council or similarly named investigative group to look into complaints about prosecutors. Local and state bar associations also have procedures for investigating complaints and taking appropriate actions. Attorneys may be disbarred or reprimanded by the State Supreme Court in many states.

Most states have Judicial Conduct Commissions to investigate judicial misconduct.

The State Attorney General's office is usually willing to investigate professional misconduct on the part of employees of the State.

If you use these avenues, be sure that you have your facts straight before filing a complaint.

CONCLUSION

Becoming an active player in the criminal justice system can add stress to your grief. You may decide that you aren't up to it and choose to let justice take its own course without your involvement. On the other hand, working with your case may be an essential component in your emotional pilgrimage to get better.

Some say that regardless of the outcome, participating in the criminal justice system gave them a sense of completeness. It will not cause you to grieve any less or erase the horror of your loved one's killing. But it may give you some sense of accomplishment.

Chapter 12

The final disposition of the case can provide a historical perspective that will enable you to focus less on the offender and more on yourself and your journey toward feeling better about life.

NOTES

XIII

FINANCIAL ISSUES

Those first few days after my daughter's murder, I remember feeling that people only wanted our money. Everywhere we went, we were asked for cash and nobody seemed to care why we were there.

> Wanda Lawendel Bincer,
> whose daughter and
> son-in-law were murdered

The financial outlay required when a loved one has been killed can be a secondary victimization. It is unfair that you should have to pay both emotionally and financially for someone else's malicious or negligent act. This chapter provides information about financial assistance after a loved one is killed. However, it is not intended to be a substitute for experienced financial advisement or legal advice.

Funeral expenses, final medical bills, travel and telephone expenses, and lost wages may leave you feeling powerless and enraged. If the person killed was a primary source of family income, immediate financial assistance may be critical.

Fortunately, others can help you with your financial matters. Do not hesitate to call on other responsible family members, trusted friends, or a professional financial advisor for help.

Chapter 13

The first step is to locate the will, insurance policies, trusts, tax returns, checkbooks, bank accounts, and information about stocks, bonds and real estate. Check desks, file cabinets, and safe deposit boxes.

In order to complete the filing of various claims for financial recovery after a death, request at least twelve *original* copies of certified death certificates from the funeral home or the probate court. If your spouse was killed, copies of the marriage license or certificate, military discharge papers, social security numbers of all family members, and birth certificates of minor children will be needed to collect benefits.

Banks

The easiest way to access cash is from checking and savings accounts, money market funds, certificates of deposit, mutual funds, stocks, and bonds. Be aware however, that penalties may be imposed if you use this money prematurely. All banks must be notified immediately upon the death of your loved one. No one will have access to these accounts until an administrator is appointed. If spouses held a joint account, the surviving spouse will have access up to a certain amount. The name on the account will need to be changed. If a joint account holds a large sum of money, a waiver may be signed to get access to the money.

A safe deposit box rented jointly or in the name of the deceased is sealed at the time of death. Requests for access to insurance policies or other legal documents must be signed and witnessed.

Social Security/Veterans Benefits

These benefits are available to survivors to replace, in part, family earnings when a wage earner is killed.

A surviving dependent spouse can collect the deceased's full social security retirement benefits at the age of 65, or reduced benefits at age 60. Unmarried children may collect benefits if they are under 18 or if they are 19 and are still in school.

A small death benefit to assist with funeral expenses is also available. Notify the Social Security Administration and the Veteran's Administration, where applicable, promptly. It may be possible to file a claim by telephone, but going in person is usually more effective. The address of the nearest Social Security office will be listed in the phone book, or you may call 1-800-772-1213. . The Veterans' Administration may be notified at Washington, D.C., 20420, or you may contact the nearest local VA office or call 1-800-827-1000.

If the person killed was already drawing Social Security or Veterans Assistance and a check written to him or her arrives after the death, you must return it. If it is made out to the deceased and the surviving spouse jointly, the spouse may take it to the nearest office and it will be stamped so it can be cashed.

Life and Medical Insurance Policies

The money from a life insurance death benefit, payable to a specific beneficiary, should be immediately and automatically available to the beneficiary, even if premiums were not paid after the death. However, delays are not unusual, especially if suicide is being considered as the cause of death.

All policies should be read carefully prior to filing claims. Some life insurance policies include double or triple indemnity benefits if the insured died catastrophically. Many policies include an "incontestability clause" that states the insurance company cannot dispute the validity of a policy after it has been in force for a specified period.

Check everywhere that records of the deceased may have been stored to be sure all policies are located. Contact the family attorney, stockbroker, financial planner, banker, accountant, and employer. Millions of insurance dollars go uncollected every year because no one knew about the policies. In addition to policies related to employment, some unions and professional organizations offer group life and/or health insurance to their members. Carefully examine health and hospital policies to be sure you know how to file claim for payment of final medical expenses.

If the person killed or injured was in a vehicular crash, the driver's automobile insurance should pay most of the medical bills. The victim's health care plan should pick up the remainder.

After all policies of the deceased have been located and examined, notify each insurance company of the death and request appropriate forms. Then check any other existing policies in which the deceased was named as a beneficiary to change the beneficiary name. The names on automobile insurance policies will also need to be changed.

Employer Benefits

Sometimes surviving family members do not know about employer policies because the policies are not stored in the home. Question the benefits specialist in the personnel department of the victim's employer about all benefits, sick leave, accrued vacation time, unpaid bonuses and the final paycheck. Ask when you should expect to receive the money. If the deceased was covered by an employer-funded pension plan, you may be entitled to monthly payments or a lump sum payment that can be rolled over into an IRA. Death benefits from 401(K) or 401(b) plans, tax-sheltered annuities or Keogh plans (self-employed) typically are paid out in a lump sum and can be rolled over into a tax-free

IRA by the surviving spouse. Other benefits will be taxed.

If dependents are covered on the health insurance policy, determine how long the coverage will continue. If coverage does not continue after a certain date, ask about options for a continuation policy for dependents under COBRA. You must apply for these extended benefits within 60 days, so timing is crucial. You must pay the entire premium plus an administrative fee up to 2%.

Also check with the deceased's *former* employers to see if benefits such as pensions are available.

If the surviving spouse is employed, his or her policies should be checked. The deceased may also have been covered by those policies. After all claims relative to a death are filed, a new beneficiary will have to be named. Check all health policies to see if mental health counseling is paid for in the event it is needed.

Get clarification from your own employer about how your time away from the office will be documented and paid. You may need time off from work to visit attorneys, attend court hearings, and the multitude of other matters that must be handled during working hours. Ask if a subpoena is required if you are attending court, or if you will be penalized for time away from your job.

In most states, the family of an employee killed on the job is entitled to worker's compensation benefits. Inquire about this as well.

Creditor Intervention

The unanticipated death of a family member nearly always means that ongoing bills will be set aside while immediate expenses are paid. Contacting creditors about the family crisis can be very difficult.

If the person killed was an income producer for the family, check all loan contracts, mortgages, and credit card contracts to see if there is a clause that pays the balance in case of death. The common language of these funds is credit or mortgage life insurance. If this is noted, notify the creditor immediately and request claim forms.

Next, list all creditors, their addresses, and the amount owed. Then consider the amount remaining after paying immediate expenses. Determine how much ongoing income and insurance money is expected. Be cautious about accepting inadequate insurance settlements out of fear of facing creditors.

From these figures, determine how much, if anything, can be paid on bills in the near future. Write each creditor. Explain what has happened and advise the company about how much you can pay each month and when payment can be expected. State that you wish to agree to a new payment schedule that will fit both your needs and the creditor's, and that if you do not hear otherwise, you will assume that the creditor agrees with the plan you have submitted.

In cases of joint accounts, inform creditors that the name on the account should be changed to your name. A surviving spouse should not assume credit cards in the name of the deceased spouse only. Credit card companies are persistent in requesting widows and widowers to sign their spouse's debts over.

In some cases, emergency funds are available for bills. Public utilities such as the electric, gas or water company may extend credit if an application is completed.

In the event that a landlord is uncooperative, phone City Hall to ask for a copy of the City's Landlord/Tenant regulations. Most legal aid services also have summaries of these regulations.

It is to the creditor's advantage to work out payment schedules so he is eventually reimbursed. It is also against the law in most states for a creditor to harass or intimidate a debtor. If the creditor refuses to accept the payment plan, write another letter and send a copy to your attorney. If that fails, ask a legal aid service or attorney, hired on an hourly rate basis, to intervene.

If a trusted friend or relative is willing, ask him or her to handle all bills for a while. These bills can seem like another wave of victimization. Decide when you are ready to resume responsibility for your financial affairs.

Automobile Insurance Benefits

Insurance practices differ from state to state. If residing in a no-fault state, costs are covered by the policy of each individual involved in the crash. This holds true even if the driver was driving someone else's vehicle. Check your state insurance code or call your State Insurance Commission at the State Capitol for defined coverage time and dollar limits. In addition to death benefits, property benefits, medical benefits, and funeral costs, inquire about the use of a rental car, wage loss, replacement costs of services such as child care and housekeeping, and mental health counseling benefits.

For injured survivors, inquire about lost wages, rehabilitation, and "replacement services," such as child care or housecleaning as well as medical benefits.

In a non no-fault state, if the driver of an automobile was liable for the crash and has liability insurance, you probably will receive benefits from the liability insurance company. Eligibility conditions vary based on the insurance law in each state.

If the driver liable for the crash had no liability insurance at the time of the crash, you may be eligible to receive benefits from the uninsured/underinsured motorist provisions of the decedent's policy. Again, the insurance laws of each state will define that eligibility.

Insurance adjustors may approach you soon after the crash. Decisions made at that time may have far-reaching financial ramifications. Be cautious.

- If you have chosen to retain a civil attorney, refer all insurance representatives to your attorney. This includes the adjustor of your own insurance company.

- If you choose to handle the claim on your own, be sure you know the company of the adjustor with whom you are speaking. If an adjustor comes to your home, ask to see a business card. If the adjustor's language is confusing, say so. Even though you may discuss the case, it is wise not to give signed or recorded statements.

- Be fully competent and aware when you discuss the case with an insurance adjustor. Grieving can make you feel numb and confused. It can cause you to have poor memory. If you are not able to discuss the case rationally with the adjustor, ask him or her to return at another time. It is a good idea to have a trusted person with you when you discuss these matters.

- Keep copies of crash reports, repair estimates, medical and funeral bills, and copies of any letters relating to the insurance settlement in a separate insurance file.

- Get several estimates on damages to the vehicle before settling on property damage. These may be obtained from body shops or automobile dealers. You can negotiate the insurer's offer if you have several estimates.

- Obtain copies of all medical bills before settling on the medical or bodily injury damages. If others in your family survived the crash, it is very important to know the full extent of injury and prognosis for treatment before making a final settlement. This may take months. Keep a daily record of adverse effects of the crash, including psychological impact. Be sure that when doctors write medical assessments, they understand the injured victim's job description, employment history, and education.

- As you discuss the insurance settlement, the company may alter their offer. Request a copy of each settlement offer in writing to avoid confusion or conflicting information. This does not need to be a formal typewritten letter, but may be handwritten, signed, and dated by the person making the offer.

- The adjustor may or may not be able to advise you of your claim rights based on statutory insurance law, since adjustors do not have legal degrees. You may ask to have a written copy of claim rights in your state. Be sure you know the statute of limitations for personal injury and property damage actions in your state. You may want to consult an attorney on an hourly fee basis for this information.

If you feel you are not being treated appropriately by a claims adjustor, contact his or her supervisor. If that is not satisfactory, write a personal and confidential letter to the president of the insurance company explaining what has happened. Your State Insurance Commission or State Board of Insurance may also be contacted. All legitimate insurance companies are regulated by a State Insurance Commission. Contact the switchboard at your State Capitol for the phone number. All telephone or personal communication relative to a complaint should be followed with a written letter. If your insurer stops paying your bills, you may need to sue your own carrier.

In many states, insurance companies are required by statute to act in "good faith." In such states, this means that if claims are unreasonably denied, if valid claims are not promptly paid, or if victim families are coerced into settling for less than is due them, this behavior gives rise to a course of action against the insurance company. Punitive damages may also be recoverable upon proof of actual malice, fraud, or oppression, usually referred to as "outrageous conduct."

Homeowner's or Renter's Insurance

Your homeowner's or renter's insurance probably will cover the loss of content from the home or, if a vehicular crash, from the car including luggage, purses or damaged clothing. These items likely will be subject to a deductible. Contact your insurer to learn how to apply for reimbursement. Usually an itemized list of lost or damaged items, age, and approximate purchase price is required.

Umbrella Liability Insurance

If the offender has an umbrella policy, it will pay for damages that extend beyond the liability limits of homeowners, renter, or automobile policies. They usually carry a maximum of $1 million in coverage, but you probably will have to file a lawsuit to get the money.

Civil Suits

If the person responsible for the death of your loved one has substantial income or assets which are recoverable, or if the liability insurance company has failed to offer a fair settlement for a claim, consider filing a wrongful death civil suit.

Civil actions are separate from the criminal case. While the State provides a prosecutor to try the criminal case, an attorney for a civil proceeding must be retained. Do not expect either attorney to advise on the other suit, although they should be interested in each other's case to enhance their own. Civil actions depend largely on the way in which the death occurred and the financial expenses incurred. Recovery of medical, funeral and property expenses are usually the first to come to mind. Financial recovery may be possible for more remote damages such as past and future wage loss including retirement benefits, and past and future pain and suffering. In some states, if one spouse is killed, the other spouse can sue for loss of consortium (change in relationship). Some states also allow for punitive damages, additional money to punish the offender.

If a public entity such as the city, county or state government was responsible in any way for the death through commission or negligence, financial recovery may be possible from them as well. Traditionally, governments have been immune from civil suits. Referred to as "sovereign immunity challenges," appellate courts in a number of jurisdictions have now found them responsible for such things as inappropriate parole release, inadequate probation supervision, and failure to arrest a drunk driver who later kills someone.

In drunk driving cases, "dram shop" statutes and case law allow for the drinking establishment that negligently encouraged an intoxicated person to continue drinking, or served a person under the age of twenty-one, to be sued if that person later harms or kills another person.

To pursue any of these sources of financial recovery, you

will need to hire a civil attorney. Take the following points into consideration:

- Shop around. A good recommendation from another victim is often an invaluable piece of information. Interview more than one attorney before making a decision. As you interview, ask what kind of cases they handle, how they charge, and what they think about your case. Tell them you will make the decision to retain at a later date. Remember, however, that the degree of success the attorney has in pursuing a full and fair outcome often depends on investigating the case as soon as possible after the crime was committed.

- Look for an attorney who concentrates a significant percentage of his practice on personal injury and wrongful death cases. If you use another type of attorney, note when you look at the contract whether additional fees will be required if co-counsel is retained.

- Ask if the attorney has more experience representing plaintiffs or defendants. Ask what percentage of his trials he has won, and what percentage of cases was settled out of court. This will help you analyze how much trial experience the attorney has, which is important. However, the vast majority of lawsuits are settled out of court and do not go to trial.

- Ask for an explanation, in terms you can understand, of the laws in your state that relate to your case, including the statute of limitations. This filing time limit varies by state from 6 months to 6 years. Ask for a brief written summary of the merits of the case as the attorney sees it at that point. This will prevent confusion later. Be skeptical, however, of an attorney who promises certain results. Airtight cases simply don't exist.

- Be sure you understand the fee schedule. Does the attorney require a retainer fee for investigating the case? Does he work on a contingency basis (paid a percentage of the actual recovery)? Does he do any work at an hourly rate? Does he require a promissory note as security for fees? If handling your case on a contingency basis, does the percentage differ if settled out of court, if going to trial, or if going to appeal? Will you be billed for out-of-pocket expenses (court fees, deposition fees) as they occur or will they accumulate until a settlement is reached? If the case is lost, are costs or fees still owed?

- Negotiating on fees, carried forth in honest good faith, is professionally acceptable and legal in most states. If state law regulates percentages, the attorney should explain the statute to you.

- If negotiable, you may want to discuss an hourly-fee for work on recovery of actual damages, and a contingency percentage that decreases as the amount of recovery for punitive damages increases. If there is no significant dispute on liability or damages, and only the insurance is recoverable, a contingency fee may be more than fair for hours involved. The attorney may therefore work for your insurance recovery on an hourly basis.

- Be sure the employment contract to retain the attorney includes the fee schedule, is complete, specific, and clearly understood before you sign it.

- Ask the attorney for copies of all correspondence relating to your case, and request that he instruct the defendant and/or his insurance company to make all offers for settlement in writing.

- Request that bills for services be itemized and match them with the fee agreement.

- Ask for receipts indicating payment and purpose of payment each time you pay your attorney.

If you have exercised care in choosing your attorney, you will probably be satisfied with his services. Negligence in civil cases is exceedingly complex and open to a variety of interpretations. This short discussion can in no way provide information sufficient to understand the intricacies of your particular case. Only your attorney can do that. Sometimes it is impossible for attorneys to give clear and concise opinions about their cases.

If you become dissatisfied, you should discuss your concerns with the attorney. If a satisfactory relationship cannot be achieved, the attorney may be discharged. At the point of discharge, the attorney will be entitled to a fee for services rendered in keeping with the terms of the employment contract.

If you suspect that your attorney's conduct is unethical, you may file a complaint with the local bar association. State Supreme Courts may also disbar, suspend, or censure an attorney for unprofessional conduct. If you wish to take legal action against your attorney, be certain of your facts.

If you win a civil case or settle favorably, plan carefully how you will use the money to avoid excessive taxes. If a large lump sum is received, invest it wisely. You may want to temporarily place it in an interest-bearing bank account, money market or other safe but accessible accounts until you can consult with a financial advisor. Eventually, you should consider investing in longer-term stocks, bonds, and tax-deferred retirement plans or IRAs.

Financial Issues

The larger the judgment or settlement, the more likely the offender may offer it as a structured settlement of perhaps a monthly payment over a period of time. While actual damages such as medical care, funeral benefits, lost wages, and pain and suffering are not taxed, punitive damages are. Because tax implications can be complicated, it would be wise to consult a tax attorney or financial advisor to help you make the best decision.

Bankruptcy

Bankruptcy Law is complex. Civil attorneys sometimes tell their clients prematurely that there is no value in filing a civil suit against an offender because even if he is found liable, he will file bankruptcy to avoid payment. That may or may not be true. Bankruptcy law is federal and changes have taken place during recent years to assure that criminals, including drunk drivers, cannot file personal bankruptcy under chapter 7 and 13 of the Bankruptcy Code to avoid civil judgments or to escape paying criminal restitution.

Bars and restaurants sued for irresponsibility serving those already intoxicated or those under the age of 21 may still file for corporate bankruptcy under Chapter 11.

If your civil attorney suggests that the offender may file bankruptcy, ask him to consult with a qualified bankruptcy attorney. The American Bar Association and most State Bar associations have bankruptcy sections that can refer you to qualified attorneys.

Crime Victim Compensation

All states, the District of Columbia and the Virgin Islands have Crime Victim Compensation programs that reimburse crime victim families for out of pocket, non-property expenses. These funds were designed for victims in which employer benefits, insurance, and civil recovery are not possible. Benefits include funeral expenses, medical expenses, loss of wages, and other financial needs deemed reasonable. In some states, dependents are eligible for lump sum benefits. All states with Victim Compensation programs provide for mental health counseling for injured victims and some pay for counseling for the survivors of someone killed. Many states provide emergency funds which are available within a few weeks of the date of the crime.

Since regulations vary from state to state, it is wise to call the prosecutor, the police department, or a local victim group such as MADD, The Bell Campaign, or Parents of Murdered Children to request a Victim Compensation application. If you are still unable to learn about the program, call the switchboard of your State Capitol and ask to be connected to the person in charge of the Crime Victim Compensation Program in your state.

The crime must be reported to the police within three to five days, and the victim family must cooperate with law enforcement officials in the prosecution of the case. However, you can collect compensation even if the case is not prosecuted.

If you are having difficulty with funeral expenses, inform your funeral director that you will be applying for Victim Compensation to cover the funeral expenses. He may then be willing to forego billing for the funeral for the time being.

You will be expected to submit bills or receipts with the application. Except for emergency awards, applications take weeks or months to process, so application procedures should be started as soon as possible. Additional bills may be submitted later. If your claim is denied or you think the award is inadequate, you have the right to appeal.

Total maximum benefits range from $10,000 to $50,000,

but if you collect compensation and later collect insurance or win a civil suit, you will be required to pay back the compensation to the state.

Restitution

Restitution is money or services ordered by the criminal court to be paid by the offender directly to the victim or surviving family after final conviction. The purpose of restitution is to make the offender personally accountable for his crime and to restore, in part, the victim's loss.

Victim requests for restitution can cover medical and funeral expenses, lost wages, ongoing counseling fees for survivors, or other expenses considered reasonable by the court. Requests for restitution must be accompanied by bills or receipts and should be presented to the criminal court judge through the prosecutor or probation department prior to sentencing of the offender. Restitution requests are usually attached to the presentence investigation prepared by the probation department.

While restitution is a very sound concept, it is not a quick or easy solution to financial stress. It is dependent upon conviction of the offender, which rarely occurs until months or years after the crime was committed. Offenders sometimes have limited income from which to pay restitution, especially if they are sent to prison. Procedures for the collection of restitution from the offender, and transferring it to the victim are rarely adequate. Once the offender is out of the criminal justice system, a means for monitoring the payments no longer exists.

Most states now require that restitution be ordered unless the judge states in the record the reasons for not doing so. A few states automatically attach a civil lien to the criminal judgment in order to assure payment after the criminal case is closed.

In most cases, unless a substantial lump sum restitution is ordered immediately following trial (which will only happen if the offender has the means to pay), chances of actually receiving restitution are slim. The court can revoke probation or parole for failure to pay restitution, but it must be recommended by the offender's probation or parole officer. If restitution is not paid in full by the time the offender leaves the criminal justice system, the remainder may be converted to a civil judgment in some states.

State and County Social Services

Families with limited income and resources that are faced with the death of a loved one, may be eligible for emergency short-term assistance from county social service agencies. This assistance may include vouchers for rent, utilities, food, and medication but rarely cash.

When a wage earner is killed, the parent of dependent children may qualify for Aid to Families with Dependent Children (AFDC) and should apply at the local State Department of Human Services or equivalent agency. Food stamps are also available for low income, low resource families. It usually takes several weeks to obtain AFDC or food stamps.

Local charities and churches willing to help may be identified through a call to United Way or local crisis hotlines. Victim witness programs and victim support groups may also be aware of financial resources.

A Final...But Very Important...Reminder:

Try to refrain from making any unnecessary major financial decisions until a year or more after your loved one's death. It is usually best to leave money where it is unless it becomes crucial to pay bills. Money taken out and not rolled over into an

IRA is generally taxed. Especially beware of unsolicited advice from investment sales people who may contact you. Decisions about significant revisions of your will, moving, investments, or sale of properties, for example, are better considered after your life has settled down a bit and after your capacity for clear and rational thinking has been restored. Don't wait too long, though, to re-draft your will to reflect new beneficiaries.

NOTES

XIV

<u>CONCLUSION</u>

Five to ten percent of our population loses a family member to death every year. Too many of these—deaths are the result of unanticipated violence.

One of the wonders of most human beings is their basic, inherent tendency to recover from the effects of trauma. Yet recovery is never complete after a loved one has been senselessly killed. Sorrow, anger, and frustration with injustice following such a death causes pain that is treatable, but difficult to cure. Time is a significant component. Grief work cannot be "pushed through." It is to be experienced little by little over time.

As family and friends of the deceased strive to refocus their sight on life rather than death, they often take one step forward, then two steps backward as they progress on this difficult journey. Grief spasms may continue for a lifetime. Many are astounded at the eruption of grieving when they least expect it.

It is hoped that this book will help victims and survivors feel free to express their feelings, choose how and when they will work on feeling better, and to discard, without guilt, the ill advice of those who care but do not understand.

It is hoped that the suggestions offered will help survivors realize that getting better means talking about what has happened. It means finding safe, supportive people with whom to share the pain. It means being patient with themselves when progress is slow. It means finding positive things to do. It also means believing that some thread of good can come from the ashes of despair.

Successful care-giving to families enduring a sudden death, whether from loving family members, friends, volunteer victim advocates, or professional counselors, requires a gentle spirit and a great deal of patience.

It is hoped that readers undertaking the task of care giving have learned to be more effective. Helping means being a good listener. It means refraining from being judgmental. It means avoiding clichés that attempt to talk victims out of their feelings of despair. It means reaching out in tangible ways, especially on holidays and anniversaries. It means talking fondly of memories of the deceased loved one. It means assertively guiding victims through the criminal justice process and advocating financially for them, if necessary.

Most significantly, however, it is hoped that those individuals who have been forced into pain they did not ask for and did not deserve will feel less alone and better understood than they did before. Walking in the shoes of a fellow struggler has a healing power all its own. Knowing that someone else understands something of their journey and genuinely cares is a gift to be treasured.

NOTES

RESOURCES . ORGANIZATIONS

National Victim Advocacy Organizations

These organizations provide information and referral services to assist victims in locating their nearest local program and offer current updates on victim rights public policy issues.

Bell Campaign (Gunshot Survivors)
San Francisco General Hospital
San Francisco, CA 94110
1-800-RIN-GING
415-821-5811 (fax)
victimresources@bellcampaign.org

Mothers Against Drunk Driving (MADD)
http://www.madd.org
511 E. John Carpenter Fwy. #700
Irving, TX 75062
1-800-GET-MADD

National Center for Victims of Crime
http://www.ncvc.org
2111 Wilson Blvd. #300
Arlington, VA 22201
703-276-2880
703-276-2889 (fax)

National Institute for Mental Health
http://www.nih.gov
5600 Fishers Lane
Rockville, MD 20857
301-496-4000

Resources

NOVA (National Organization for Victim Assistance)
http://www.try-nova.org
1757 Park Road NW
Washington, D.C. 20004
202-393-NOVA

National Sheriff's Association (Victim Program)
http://www.sheriffs.org
1450 Duke Street
Alexandria, VA 22314
703-836-7837 / 1-800-424-7827

Office for Victims of Crime
http://www.ojp.usdoj.gov/ovc/
U.S. Department of Justice
810 Seventh Street NW
Washington, D.C. 20531
202-307-5983
202-305-2446 (fax)

Office for Victims of Crime Resource Center
http://www.ncjrs.org
Box 6000
Rockville, MD 20849-6000
1-800-627-6872

Samaritans (Suicide)
500 Commonwealth Avenue
Boston, MA 02215
617-247-0220 (24 hours)
617-247-8050 (Teens)

Victims of Crime Resource Center
McGeorge School of Law

University of the Pacific
3200 Fifth Avenue
Sacramento, CA 95817
1-800-VIC-TIMS (Calif.)
916-739-7049

National Victim Support Organizations
These organizations refer to local support groups and provide other services for families of those killed.

Compassionate Friends
P.O. Box 3696
Oakbrook, IL 60522-3696
708-990-0010

Concerns of Police Survivors (COPS)
http://www.nationalcops.org
P.O. Box 3199
South Highway Five
Camdenton, MO 65020
573-346-4911
573-346-1414 (fax)

Parents of Murdered Children
http://www.pomc.com
100 E. 8th Street, B-41
Cincinnati, OH 45202
513-721-LOVE
513-345-4489 (fax)

Tragedy Assistance Program for Survivors (TAPS)
(Military Deaths)
http://www.taps.org
2001 "S" Street NW, #300
Washington, D.C. 20009

Resources
1-800-959-TAPS
202-639-5312 (fax)

National Trauma and Bereavement Counseling
Organizations

American Psychological Association
http://www.apa.org/ptsd.html
750 First Street NE
Washington, D.C. 22002-4242
202-336-5500

Association for Death Education and Counseling
(ADEC)
342 North Main Street
West Hartford, CT 06117-2507
860-586-7503
860-586-7550 (fax)
info@adec.org

Association of Traumatic Stress Specialists
http://www.atts-hq.com
7338 Broad River Road
Irmo, South Carolina 29063
803-781-0017
803-781-3899 (fax)
tidwell@netside.com

Center for Loss and Life Transition
3735 Broken Bow Road
Ft. Collins, CO 80526
970-226-6050
970-226-6051 (fax)

The International Society for Traumatic Stress Studies
http://www.istss.org
60 Revere Drive
Suite 500
Northbrook, IL 60062
847-480-9028
847-480-9282

National Resources for Civil Suits

American Trial Lawyers Association
1050 31st Street NW
Washington, D.C. 20007
202-965-3500

Trial Lawyers for Public Justice, P.C.
1625 Massachusetts Avenue S. 100
Washington, D.C. 20036
202-797-8600

Victim's Assistance Legal Organization
(VALOR)
8180 Greensboro Drive, #1070
McLean, VA 22102-3823
703-748-0811
703-356-5085 (fax)
valorino@cvols.com

National Insurance Organizations

Alliance of American Insurers
1501 Woodfield Road, Suite 400 West
Schaumberg, IL 60173-4980

Resources
847-330-8500

National Association of Independent Insurers
http://www.naii.org
2600 River Road
Des Plaines, IL 60018
847-297-7800

National Medical Resources

American College of Emergency Physicians
1125 Executive Circle
Irving, TX 75038
972-550-0911

American Trauma Society
1400 Mercantile Lane
Suite 188
Landover, MD 20785
1-800-556-7890

National Head Injury Foundation
1776 Massachusetts Avenue NW, #100
Washington, D.C. 20036
1-800-444-NHIF
202-296-8850 (fax)

Spinal Cord Society
Rt. 5, Box 22A, Wendell Road
Fergus Falls, MN 56537
218-739-5252

National Funeral/Burial Organizations

National Funeral Directors Association
11121 West Oklahoma Avenue
Milwaukee, WI 53227
414-604-2870
(FISCAP – arbitrates consumer complaints)

National Faith-Based Victim Organizations

Neighbors Who Care
1856 Old Reston Avenue
Reston, VA 20190
1-800-692-7770
1-703-904-7311

Additional Victim Resources

National Crime Victim's Research and Treatment
Center
http://www.musc.edu/cvc/
Medical University of South Carolina
165 Cannon Street
PO Box 250852
Charleston, SC 29425
843-792-2945
843-792-3388 (fax)

Partnership Against Violence Network (PAVNET)
http://www.pavnet.org
10301 Baltimore Avenue

Beltsville, MD 20705
301-504-5462
jgladsto@nalusda.gov

Violence Against Women's Office (VAWO)
http://www.usdoj.gov/vawo/index.html
810 7th Street NW
Washington, D.C. 20531
202-616-8894
202-307-3911 (fax)
bcampbel@justice.usdoj.gov

Bereavement and Hospice Support Netline
http://www.ubalt.edu/www/bereavement

Findlaw
http://www.findlaw.com/

GriefNet
http://www.rights.org/deathnet

Higher Education Center Against Violence and Abuse
http://www.umn.edu/mincava/

State Law and Legislative Information
http://lawlib.wuacc.edu/washlaw/uslaw/statelaw.html

Suicide Prevention Advocacy Network
http://www.spanusa.org

U.S. Supreme Court Decisions
http://supct.law.cornell.edu/supct/

Resources

Index

Index

Index